Lost Restaurants OF NAPA VALLEY AND Their Recipes

Lost Restaurants OF NAPA VALLEY AND Their Recipes

ALEXANDRIA BROWN

AMERICAN PALATE

Published by American Palate
A Division of The History Press
Charleston, SC
www.historypress.com

Copyright © 2020 by Alexandria Brown
All rights reserved

Back cover, inset: Jonesy's special potatoes courtesy of the author, 2019.

First published 2020

Manufactured in the United States

ISBN 9781467144612

Library of Congress Control Number: 2019956024

Notice: The information in this book is true and complete to the best of our knowledge. It is offered without guarantee on the part of the author or The History Press. The author and The History Press disclaim all liability in connection with the use of this book.

All rights reserved. No part of this book may be reproduced or transmitted in any form whatsoever without prior written permission from the publisher except in the case of brief quotations embodied in critical articles and reviews.

To my mom, who puts up with a lot and loves me anyway.

Contents

Preface	9
Acknowledgements	11
PART I. THE EARLY DAYS OF EATING OUT	13
1. Empire Saloon	15
2. Dorr's Saloons	18
3. Valley House Restaurant	22
PART II. "THE LUSCIOUS BIVALVE"	25
4. Arcade Restaurant	29
5. The Nielsens' Restaurants	32
PART III. ROOM AND BOARD	37
6. Exchange and French Restaurants	41
7. Napa Hotel	43
8. Magnolia Hotel (Calistoga)	49
9. Aetna Springs Resort	53
PART IV. CHILI QUEENS AND TAMALE MEN	59
10. Tamale Parlors	63
11. Dabner Brothers Restaurant	67
12. Spanish Restaurant	69
13. El Faro Restaurant	72

Contents

PART V. CHOW CHOP SUEY	77
14. Lai Hing Company	79
15. Sang Wo's Lunch Counter	84
16. A-1 Cafe	87
PART VI. LITTLE ITALY	95
17. The Depot	99
18. Napa Raviola and Noodle Parlor	107
PART VII. EARLY TWENTIETH-CENTURY CLASSICS	111
19. Mrs. Tobin's Restaurants	113
20. Classic Grill	117
PART VIII. MID-CENTURY MODERN	125
21. Jonesy's Famous Steak House	129
22. Taylor's Refresher	135
23. Palby's	143
PART IX. RESTAURANT RENAISSANCE	149
24. Magnolia Hotel (Yountville)	151
Bibliography	161
Index	185
About the Author	191

Preface

Some of my fondest memories from childhood are tied to food—my mom teaching me how to make cornbread, sneaking popcorn into the Cinedome, school lunches of haystacks and vegetarian corn dogs, church potlucks, a slice of pizza from Papa Joe's after piano lessons, Saturday afternoon lunch at Marie Callender's. Food brings us together as family, as friends, as a community, but rarely do we think about where that food came from. We do not often consider the people who grew and harvested the ingredients, the cooks who prepared it, the staff who served it, the restaurateur who manages the business, the first people who invented the original dish and the people who appropriated it into something else.

While researching this book, many Napans shared with me their stories about their favorite restaurants: the librarian who still mourned the loss of First Squeeze, the local history lovers who told tales of the Shrimp Boat, the Swiss-Italian immigrant who favored the Grape Vine Inn, the seniors who fondly recalled whiling away their teen years at the Wright Spot and more. There was simply no way to include every restaurant from Napa County's beginnings until today without producing a multivolume series thousands of pages in length. Instead, the eateries herein represent some of the culinary trends that had the greatest impact on the county. This book will reveal the origins of some of our most beloved dishes, shed light on the people who cooked and served them and explore how the history of Napa County's cuisine informs our present and shapes our future.

Acknowledgements

This book would not have been possible without the assistance and contributions of the following: Beverly Brown Healey, Diane R. Adams, John L. Callan, Rick Curry, Craig and Jeannine Graffin, Jeanette Mulgrew, Herman Soon and Cheryl Fielder, Jean and Tom Nicholson of the Taylor family, Todd L. Shulman, Kimberly Wilkinson, Robert Zeller, Breanna Feliciano of Napa County Library, Kathy Bazzoli, Gail Sharpsteen and Bev Barnes of the Sharpsteen Museum, Lawrence Rodriguez of the Office of the Assessor and County Clerk/Recorder, the Offices of the County Clerk and the Hall of Records, St. Helena Historical Society, California State Library, the Huntington Library and the hardworking staff and volunteers at Napa County Historical Society.

I also want to thank the Nichelini family—particularly Doug and Kay Patterson, Dorothy Hoffman, Diane Patterson and Leona Marini—for their support.

And extra special thanks to my dedicated research assistant Oliver.

PART I

THE EARLY DAYS OF EATING OUT

In the 1880s, historian Hubert Howe Bancroft ruminated on the state of restaurants in California: "The best are kept by foreigners, Germans, French, Italians; American restaurants are invariably second, third, or fourth rate. The typical American can keep a hotel such as no foreigner may hope to equal, but when it comes to restaurant-feeding, the tables are turned." Why this disparity? Bancroft believed it was because "the American hotel is an American institution, while the restaurant is as fully European." While it is true that many immigrants, European or otherwise, worked in California's food service industry, which group made the better restaurateur is contestable. On the origins of the restaurant, however, he was spot on.

Restaurants were born in Paris. In those early eateries, wealthy patrons unable to eat a full meal of solid food found sustenance by consuming a meat broth called a "restaurant." Meals were available at all hours rather than only during set times. Guests were seated at tables by waiters and given a menu to peruse. By the 1820s, the menus of Parisian restaurants had expanded, and the layout and functionality of the physical space was beginning to look similar to modern restaurants.

The first restaurants landed in the United States in the early nineteenth century. But it was the boom in population brought by the gold rush, urbanization and the influx of British and European immigrants that kicked off the restaurant revolution. Napa's early restaurants had one major difference from those of today: many offered sleeping quarters. In the

1850s and 1860s, the population was growing fast, and there were few permanent structures. Anyone who wanted a house had to purchase the land and acquire and assemble all the construction materials. Once it was built and furnishings and kitchen equipment purchased and installed, the entire cooking process—from procuring and storing ingredients to preparing dishes—might take several hours. This was simply unfeasible for a lot of people, especially those who were single, poor and/ or lived in urban areas or temporary encampments.

Because so many people needed somewhere to eat and a place to sleep, hotels often served meals while restaurants and saloons often offered beds. The food at a hotel might not be as good as at a restaurant, but the establishment usually had private rooms, ideal for long-term residents. Frequently, the lodging available at a restaurant or saloon were cots, bunkbeds or spaces marked off on the floor for bedrolls, but the food was generally decent. Where food was available—at a saloon, hotel, lodging or boarding house or restaurant—mattered less than whether it was affordable and edible.

Chapter 1
Empire Saloon

Nineteen-year-old Nathan Coombs arrived in Napa in 1845. At the time, what is now Napa city was divided between three Californio (Mexican citizens born and living in the Alta California region of Mexican territory) rancho owners: Nicolás Higuera, Cayetano Juárez and Colonel Salvador Vallejo, brother of General Mariano Vallejo. Napa's Indigenous people, the Wappo and Southern Patwin, mostly labored on nearby missions or ranchos that had once been their ancestral lands, although some managed to continue living in their traditional ways. Coombs was one of an increasing number of American and British immigrants encroaching on Mexican territory. He and numerous other men, many of whom would later become prominent Napans, instigated the Bear Flag Revolt in June 1846. They marched across the northern part of the county into Sonoma and imprisoned members of the Vallejo family. Then they claimed California for the United States.

Tensions were high between Mexicans and Americans as their soldiers fought in the Southwest during the Mexican-American War (1846–48). In Napa, some Californios cultivated long-standing grudges against the Americans, but nevertheless, both parties found ways to work together. When Nicolás Higuera needed a new adobe on his rancho, he hired Nathan Coombs and John Grigsby, another Bear Flagger, to build it. In lieu of cash, Coombs and Grigsby requested a plot of land planted in beans by the Napa River just north of Higuera's embarcadero (located on the riverbank at the intersection of Fifth and Division Streets). Grigsby

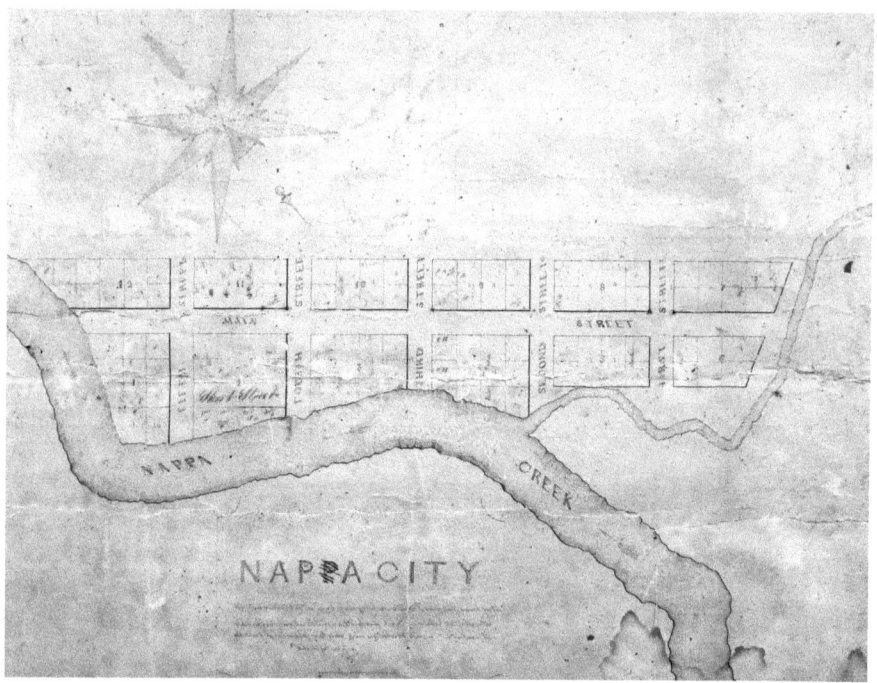

The original map of "Nappa," surveyed by Em. A. d'Hemicourt in 1847. *Courtesy of Napa County Historical Society.*

sold Coombs his share and left his partner to his own devices. In the fall of 1847, Coombs cleared the land and laid out eight square blocks (what is now Main Street from First to Fifth) and shortly thereafter founded the city of Napa.

Another Bear Flagger who settled in Napa was Pennsylvanian Harrison Pierce. He was not much older than Coombs when he came to the area in 1843 after ditching a whaling ship in Oregon. After the Revolt, he went north toward Rancho Carne Humana (near St. Helena), owned by a cantankerous English doctor named Edward Bale. Pierce was hired to oversee a sawmill belonging to another Bear Flagger, Ralph Kilburn.

In the spring of 1848, Pierce decided that what Napa really needed was a saloon. Pierce, Kilburn and William Nash—a traveler in the wagon train that split from the Donner Party before their luck went bad—milled the lumber at Kilburn's mill and carted it down to Napa. George Cornwell, a ship captain who came to Napa in 1848, told a slightly different version of this story. He claimed Pierce merely commissioned the construction and that the real work was done by two men known only as Southard and Sweezy.

They, Cornwell said, built the first permanent structure in town, and Pierce's saloon was constructed behind it.

Either way, construction moved along at a hasty pace until Pierce hit a snag. He had everything but the rafters completed on the one-and-a-half-story, eighteen-by-twenty-four-foot building before realizing he had accidentally erected it in the center of Main Street. The error seems egregious, but at the time it was an easy one to make. When Coombs surveyed the townsite, he had marked the divisions between the roads and lots with small stakes in the ground. But in the year between surveying and Pierce's construction, a thick layer of wild oats had sprouted up and smothered the stakes. The grass was mowed down and the stakes uncovered. With Higuera's help, Pierce pushed the frame to the south side of Third Street between Main Street and the river.

Pierce completed construction of the Empire Saloon in early May but almost immediately abandoned it. A few days before, California's first millionaire and the eventual founder of Calistoga Hot Springs, Samuel Brannan, stood in Portsmouth Square in San Francisco and announced the discovery of gold. Before the saloon even opened its doors, Pierce, Kilburn, six other white Americans and an Indigenous woman and her Californio husband left together to seek their fortune. They were the first of many Napans who deserted the valley for the mountains in 1848.

Like most miners, Pierce was unsuccessful in his ventures. He returned to Napa in the fall, stocked up on liquor and finally opened his saloon. By the following summer, he was offering lodging and one-dollar meals of coffee, beef and hard bread. The Empire Saloon was the site of Napa's first election in 1849 and was a well-known drinking and dining establishment for several years.

How long Pierce operated the Empire Saloon is a mystery. The sign hung at least until 1857, but the structure cycled through other uses. At some point, it was converted to a private home. The building stood as of 1881. After leaving the saloon business, Pierce remained in town doing who knows what. It seems he never married or had children; he died in 1870.

Chapter 2
Dorr's Saloons

Six years after it was founded, Napa city had about four hundred residents and forty buildings. Most of the structures were temporary, but that would soon change. With so many men, few cultural and educational offerings and a feeling of transience permeating the air, it is no wonder that Napa's most popular establishments were bars and gambling facilities. Napa had fourteen saloons, four hotels and two restaurants by 1861.

Many saloons offered food along with cigars, liquor, wine and beer. Some went a step further and provided a "free" lunch. With the purchase of a drink, a customer could enjoy a hot or cold lunch of soup, seafood and meat, or, if the saloonkeeper was particularly stingy, crackers and cheese. Much like a modern-day buffet, lunch was typically spread out on a large table, and patrons could eat as much as they wanted. The concept originated in the West and Midwest and by the late nineteenth century was common in metropolises like Chicago and New York City.

Free lunches were very popular in San Francisco Bay Area saloons during the gold rush, even if more than a few patrons took advantage of the proprietors. San Francisco saloonkeepers tried to crush the free lunch system in 1854 but failed miserably. It was later estimated that nearly five thousand people (out of a population of about thirty-six thousand) survived almost entirely on free lunches. The poor and working class were especially dependent, as it might be their only meal of the day. Many saloons in Napa city also offered free lunches, such as the Fashion Saloon, operated by John

The Early Days of Eating Out

The Europa House Saloon, William Tell Saloon and St. Helena Brewery on Main Street in St. Helena in the late nineteenth century. *Courtesy of Sharpsteen Museum.*

Cornwell. Patrons could knock back a glass of wine or liquor, puff on a cigar and dine on fresh oysters prepared in a variety of styles or a hot lunch served daily. James N. Cosgrove ran a wholesale and retail liquor store on Main Street where guests who partook of his wide selection of "pure and unadulterated liquors" had the pleasure of enjoying a free hot lunch every day starting at 10:00 a.m.

Jacob Blumer opened a saloon on Second Street near Brown in the late 1850s. Originally from Switzerland, Blumer immigrated in 1839 and made his way to Napa in the early years of the gold rush. He sold his saloon to Matthias Dorr in 1861 and eventually relocated to Green Valley just over the hills in Solano County.

Dorr came to the United States from Prussia with his father sometime before 1858. He married Annie, born in Bavaria, and the two moved to Napa, where they had at least five children. He expanded his new saloon by fifteen feet, redid the wallpaper, refurbished the interior and set up a lunch table and chop house. When he took over the Capitol Saloon on Second Street near Main in 1863, he upgraded again. Besides billiards and plenty of alcohol and cigars, Dorr served a hot lunch every day from 10:00 a.m. to 2:00 p.m. Every evening, diners partook of pigs' feet, oysters and coffee. The saloon also offered lodging by the day or week.

Inside an unknown upvalley saloon in the early twentieth century. *Courtesy of Sharpsteen Museum.*

In 1868, Dorr expanded once more and added a restaurant at the back of his saloon. It was run by French immigrant Achille Monmert, the former cook at the Revere House in Napa. Monmert operated a "superior restaurant, conducted on the French plan where travelers, transient and permanent, and other patrons, can obtain at all hours the choicest viands of the seasons served up in a superior style." The space was large enough to host balls and parties and had private rooms for women and mixed-gender get-togethers. At the time, it was considered somewhat unseemly for respectable women to dine in restaurants, so some owners erected separate dining rooms apart from the rough-and-tumble crowd of men.

Monmert also served ice cream in his restaurant. Until the mid-nineteenth century, ice cream was an expensive delicacy. Procuring enough ice in warmer climates to manufacture ice cream even on a small scale was challenging to say the least. On top of that, the equipment to produce it was cumbersome and the process difficult. Then, in 1843, an enigmatic woman named Nancy Johnson patented a revolutionary invention. All that is known of Nancy is that she may have been from Philadelphia and she was an old woman when she died in the 1890s or 1900s. But her hand-cranked ice cream freezer was the key to turning a sweet treat into an American favorite.

The Early Days of Eating Out

The Gilt Edge Saloon on Main Street, Napa, in 1906. Note the entrance to the grill below the saloon to the right. Photographer H.A. Darms. *Courtesy of Napa County Historical Society.*

Ice cream was not rare in the early 1870s, but it was difficult to come by. Only a few establishments in Napa sold it, giving the Paris Restaurant a leg up on the competition.

In 1874, a year after Annie's death, Dorr got out of the service industry for good and switched to manufacturing. He and his partner, a man known only as Brinkmann, made a tidy profit stuffing Cuban tobacco into broadleaf wrappers and then selling the resulting cigars. Since most saloons sold cigars, there was lots of demand for their supply. Dorr remained in the business until his death five years later.

Chapter 3
Valley House Restaurant

Turner G. Baxter built the earliest known restaurant in a permanent structure in Napa County. From Kentucky, Baxter left home at fifteen and ended up in New Salem, Illinois. There he learned carpentry and made friends with a grocery store clerk who later became one of the most important people in American history: Abraham Lincoln. Interestingly enough, this was not Baxter's only presidential connection; his grandfather served under George Washington during the American Revolution.

Baxter wandered around the Midwest for a while before the siren song of gold lured him west. He tried his hand at this and that for a few months and then, in November 1849, rode into Napa. He set up a grocery store and saloon before buying a steamer in 1850. The *Dolphin* was the first commercial steamboat to sail regular service between Napa and San Francisco. Before trains and paved roadways, ships were the fastest way to get to and from San Francisco, especially when transporting freight. Locals joked that because Baxter was so tall, they could see him coming around the river bend before his ship's smokestack.

About the same time as he bought his steamer, Baxter hired Pennsylvanian J.B. Horrell to construct for him a restaurant on Main Street. In 1852, Baxter sold the *Dolphin* and converted his restaurant into a hotel. Never content to remain in one place or occupation too long, he packed up and left for Valparaíso, Chile, in 1856 to run a tugboat in the harbor. That did not last long either, and he returned to Napa and opened the Valley House Restaurant on Brown Street near Second. That, too, lasted a single

THE EARLY DAYS OF EATING OUT

BILL OF FARE.
VALLEY HOUSE RESTAURANT,
BROWN STREET,
E. HARRY MOWER, · · Proprietor.

DINNER.
BREAD AND POTATOES INCLUDED.

SOUPS:
Oyster, 12½ | Veal Broth, 12½
Chicken, 12½ | Mutton Broth, 12½

FISH:
Baked Salmon, 25 | Fresh Herring, 25
Fresh Trout, 25

BOILED:
Corn Beef and Cabbage, 25 | Mutton, Caper Sauce, 25
Pigs Feet, pickeann sauce, 25 | Ham, 25
 | Tongue, 25

ROAST:
Roast Beef, 25 | Mutton, 25
Beef, a la mode, 25 | Veal, 25
Pork, 25

GAME:
Roast Turkey, Cranberry Sauce, 25 | Roast Duck, 25
Roast Chicken, Oyster Sauce, 25 | Fricassed Chicken, 25

ENTREES:
Veal and Mutton Pie, 25 | Chicken Curry, 25

RELISHES:
Worcestershire Sauce, | Gherkin Pickles,
French Mustard, | London Club,

VEGETABLES:
Sweet Potatoes, 12½ | Cold Slaw, 12½
Irish Potatoes, 12½ | Cabbage, 12½
Boiled Onions, 12½ | Cauliflower, 12½
Lima Beans, 12½

PIES:
Custard, 12 | Green Apple, 12
Squash, 12 | Grape, 12

PUDDINGS:
English Plum, 12 | Corn Starch, 12

SUPPER.
Coffee Tea or Bread, served with the following Dishes:
Tenderloin Steak, 37 | Oyster Stew, 50
Porter House Steak, 37 | Oysters in Bread, 50
Beef Steak and Onions, 25 | Oysters fried, 50
Mutton Chop, 25 | Oysters raw, 25
Sausage fried, 25 | Oysters in Batter, 50
Beef Steak a la Bourdelaise, 25 | Oysters, fancy Roast, 50
 | Eggs Boiled, (3) 37
Beef Steak, Spanish, 25 | Eggs Poached, (3) 37
Pork Steak, 25 | Eggs Scrambled, (3) 37
Liver and Onions, 25 | Egg Omelet, (3) 37
Venison Steak, 25 | French Omelet, (3) 37
Ham and Eggs, (three) 50 | Brandy Omelet, (3) 37

CAKES, WITH COFFEE OR TEA.
Hot Rolls, 15 | German Cakes, 15
English Muffins, 15 | Corn Bread, 15
Waffles, 25 | Corn Batter, 16
Flannel Cakes, 15

Single Meals, 50 Cents.

The bill of fare for the Valley House Restaurant, November 8, 1862, with E. Harry Mower as proprietor. Courtesy of the Huntington Library.

year. He stuck with sailing steamers for a bit but changed employers frequently. In the years before retiring, he took up work as a carpenter once more. Captain Baxter died in 1915 at the ripe old age of ninety-four.

Nothing is known of Baxter's first restaurant or how he ran the Valley House Restaurant. The restaurant's second proprietor, H. Sanderson, appears in no local records. However, newspaper advertisements indicate he operated on the European Plan. Meals were fifty cents, and turkey and oysters were available on demand. Patrons could rent the venue or hire Sanderson for catering balls, parties and picnics.

E. Harry Mower took over in 1862, and while there is little information about the man, there is quite a bit on the restaurant. Mower may have gone by the name Harry Moore at one point, but the historical record is unclear. He had been a cook at John Hogan's Napa Restaurant before taking over the Valley House in June. Intending to make a big splash with his new venture, Mower hosted an Independence Day dinner of lamb, chicken, duck, turkey, oyster sauce, vegetables, pastry and more. Mower's motto was "Cheap, good, and plenty."

On a normal day, fifty-cent meals and lunch were available at all hours, along with rooms for five dollars per week. The dinner menu was extensive yet affordable: oyster or chicken soup, veal or mutton broth, baked salmon, fresh trout and herring, corned beef and cabbage, pigs' feet with "pickeann sauce," muton with caper sauce, ham, beef tongue, beef à la mode, roast beef, pork, mutton, veal, duck, turkey with cranberry sauce, chicken with oyster sauce, chicken fricassee, veal and mutton pie, chicken curry, sweet potatoes, Irish potatoes, boiled onions, lima beans, "cold slaw," cabbage and cauliflower, plus relishes of Worcestershire sauce, French mustard, gherkin pickles and London club. Pies of custard, squash, green apple or grape and puddings of English plum or cornstarch were for dessert. A full dinner meal with complimentary sides of bread and potatoes cost about a buck. Supper was just as varied, with tenderloin or porterhouse steak, steak and onions or bordelaise sauce, "Beef Steak, Spanish," pork, mutton chop, fried sausage, liver and onions, venison and oysters in stew, on bread, raw, fried, in batter or "fancy roast." It also included what we think of today as breakfast foods like waffles, eggs and English muffins, as well as flannel cake, rolls, cornbread, "corn batter" and "German Cakes."

When Mower left to take over the Exchange Restaurant in 1863, it may have been the death knell for the Valley House. As of 1871, the site was occupied by a bookstore and stationery shop, although it is unclear if the store was in the same building or if the restaurant had been torn down and the store built on the spot. The Valley House Restaurant did not have a long existence, but it still helped shape Napa's dining habits.

Breakfast Biscuit
Recipe printed in the *St. Helena Star*, 1875

Take a piece of risen bread dough, and work it into one beaten egg and a teaspoonful of butter or lard; when it is thoroughly amalgamated, flour your hands and make it into balls the size of an egg; rub a tin over with milk, and set them in a quick oven for twenty minutes, and serve them hot for breakfast. When eaten, break them open; to cut would make them heavy.

Mrs. Adam's Wedding Cake
Recipe printed in the *St. Helena Star*, 1875

One pound of brown sugar, one pound of butter, one pound of flour, twelve eggs, one cup of molasses, six pounds Valentina raisins, three pounds currants, two pounds of citron, one ounce of cinnamon, one ounce of mace, one ounce of cloves, two gills of brandy, the juice and grated rind of two lemons, two nutmegs, and sufficient flour to dust the fruit.

PART II

"THE LUSCIOUS BIVALVE"

OYSTERS WERE CONSUMED BY INDIGENOUS PEOPLE FOR MILLENNIA before British and European explorers ever set foot on North American soil. It took a while for the delicacy to catch on with Americans, but by the 1850s, they were one of the most popular foods to come out of New York City. Canned, fresh, stewed, steamed, raw, in cocktails—there were infinite ways to consume the mollusk, and Americans tried them all. Americans ate so many oysters that a "war" broke out between state authorities from Maryland and Virginia and oyster pirates pillaging the Chesapeake Bay and the Potomac River.

In the mid-nineteenth century, oysters were particularly tied to saloons. When not consuming a variety of alcoholic beverages, bar-goers guzzled down oysters by the bucketful. It did not take long for restaurants to jump on the oyster bandwagon. In Napa County, oyster houses proliferated and were often paired with a lunch counter or chophouse.

In St. Helena, the Elite Saloon offered a daily special of oysters from the East Coast, as well as free lunch anytime and clams on Friday. E. Heymann had oysters on the half-shell available for Railroad House customers indulging in wine, liquor, cigars or billiards. The Arcade Saloon in Napa (no known connection to the Arcade Restaurant) offered stewed, fried and raw oysters brought up by boat from San Francisco. But A. Javon takes the cake for the most creative oyster enterprise. He ran a combination oyster saloon, coffeehouse and market selling fish and vegetables out of his business on Main Street, Napa. On Tuesdays and Fridays, he had fresh fish

Volunteer firefighters with Napa Hook and Ladder posing in front of the Pioneer Bakery Coffee House and Chop House, about 1885. *Courtesy of Napa County Historical Society.*

for sale, and shrimp, crab, lobster, oysters and other shellfish were always available. Customers ordered groceries and then stuck around for a ten-cent cup of coffee and a plate of stewed or half-shell oysters for two bits (slang for twenty-five cents).

Completed in 1869, the transcontinental railroad made it easier to ship the bivalves to the gaping maws of oyster-mad westerners. By the 1870s, oysters had been transplanted in California. The feat was so successful that the *San Francisco Daily Post* wrote, "The largest bonanza in the way of a mine must inevitably be worked out in time, but the oyster wealth of the Gulf of California is inexhaustible, as all persons who are wise enough to become stockholders will by and by find to their entire satisfaction."

Chapter 4
Arcade Restaurant

The earliest years of the Arcade Restaurant are hazy. It opened on Main Street in downtown Napa in the late 1850s or early 1860s. J.W. Davis became proprietor in the summer of 1862 and offered meals any time of day. In the advertisement where he announced he was taking over the restaurant, he also declared his intentions to establish himself in Napa; however, he seems to have been unsuccessful in both ventures. Davis appears in no official records, directories or newspaper articles except the one.

A decade later, Patrick Milton Hogan was in charge. Not much is known about him except that he was born in Ireland in about 1840. Besides the typical meals, Hogan instituted the Canal Street Plan, which he described as "you call for what you want, and pay only for what you get." Originating on Canal Street in New York City, this plan was common in oyster cellars that operated below the main saloon where the cooler temperatures kept the bivalves fresher longer. For a few cents, diners could eat as many oysters as they wanted. There were probably many oyster eateries in Napa County that relied on the Canal Street Plan, but only the Arcade Restaurant chose to advertise it in the local newspapers.

Like many of Napa's early dining establishments, the Arcade moved locations at least once. When he moved into the Sharvin Building at First and Main Streets in 1873, Hogan hung a brand-new sign that could be seen from several blocks up and down. The *Napa Register* commended him for "making himself an enduring reputation as a restaurateur in Napa. He has

The Napa City Oyster and Chop House is in the brick F. Martin Building in this 1906 H.A. Darms photo of Brown Street from Third. All except the Martin Building no longer exist; it was badly damaged in the 2014 earthquake. *Courtesy of Napa County Historical Society.*

made a creditable attempt to furnish good meals at a cheap price, and has succeeded. At his tables may be found fish, flesh and fowl and the fruits of the season." He served a wide range of dishes, everything from "a fat, juicy steak" to hot chocolate to ham and eggs to mutton broth. And, of course, oysters—as a stew, "in crumbs," on the half-shell or "fried in eggs." Anti-Chinese fervor would not reach its peak until the 1890s, but Hogan was an early participant. In 1872, he was proud to advertise that he refused to hire Chinese cooks.

At some point, Hogan gave up the Arcade and James C. Ritchie stepped in. Ritchie dreamed of getting a job at a wholesale grocery store in San Francisco, so he sold the restaurant to the Hattons in 1887. The job did not last, and Ritchie was back in town a few months later. He opened a new restaurant, the Fountain, on the east side of Main Street between First and Second. Eastern oysters and chicken dinners were one of many dishes available at "the best Eating House north of San Francisco." Rooms were also available to boarders by the week or month. Unfortunately, he filed for insolvency in 1892 when he could not pay off his debts of nearly $3,500. The Pickles took over the Fountain but lost it after two years for failing to pay rent. Eventually, the property owner, Jacob F. Schwartz, expanded his hardware store into the old restaurant, and that was the end of that.

As for the Arcade, it did well under Edward and Sabina Hatton. Edward left his home in New Bedford, Massachusetts, for California with his first wife, Susan, in the early 1850s. Once in Napa, he opened a barbershop and became one of several African American barbers in the county. Civically minded and politically active, Edward was a North Bay district representative for the California Convention of Colored Citizens (CCC), a series of conventions held between 1855 and 1865 where African Americans worked together to push for citizenship rights. At the time in California, as with most of the United States, people of color and Indigenous people were barred from many public facilities and could not testify in court, vote or attend public school. The CCC also worked with abolitionists to end slavery. Later, he became a contributor and agent for the San Francisco–based newspapers the *Pacific Appeal* and the *Elevator*, both of which were written by and for African Americans, and was among the first group of Black Napans to register to vote after the Fifteenth Amendment was ratified in 1870.

Susan passed away in the late 1860s or early 1870s, and Edward remarried, this time to widow Sabina H. Dyer. Sabina and Edward's restaurant was "open all hours of the day and evening" and kept tables "always supplied with the best the market affords." After a few months, they gave the restaurant over to Margaret E. Hatton, who may have been one of Edward's daughters or a daughter-in-law. Edward and Sabina moved back to San Francisco, where he remained until his death in 1889.

Margaret had the Arcade Restaurant less than a year before it burned to the ground in July 1888. The fire broke out at 1:00 a.m. between the restaurant and True's Saloon and spread to nearby buildings, even threatening the Napa Hotel across the street. It took four different fire companies nearly two hours to put out the flames, and when they were done, six businesses were destroyed and $10,000 in damage was done. Margaret got out of the restaurant business, and the Arcade never reopened.

Chapter 5

The Nielsens' Restaurants

John Nielsen and his wife (only her first initial, "M.," is known) opened the St. Helena Restaurant on Hunt Avenue near the railroad tracks sometime in the early 1880s. Before that, John had worked in central California and in vineyards in the upper Napa Valley. John was the proprietor and manager and his wife the cook. Operating on the European Plan, the restaurant offered rooms to let—only four dollars per week—and sold single meals for a quarter. It also had a coffee saloon.

Coffee likely originated from the Red Sea region between North Africa and the Middle East. By the mid-fifteenth century, it was a staple throughout the Islamic world as a drink that was believed to be both medically beneficial and personally enjoyable. Eventually, European and British traders stumbled upon coffee and introduced it to their home countries. Colonists spread it across their empires in North and South America and cultivated it on plantations run on Indigenous and African slave labor. As of the 1880s, the coffee beans purchased by the Nielsens came from the 100,000 or so bags shipped into San Francisco ports every year.

Coffeehouses multiplied after the United States took over territory owned by the two big coffee-drinking nations of France and Mexico through the Louisiana Purchase of 1803 and the Mexican-American War of 1846–48. The coffee saloon was not dissimilar to the coffeehouse. Proponents of temperance and prohibition saw the coffee saloon as the ideal alternative to the alcohol saloon. It was a place where men could gather and drink coffee

"THE LUSCIOUS BIVALVE"

The St. Helena Restaurant and Coffee Saloon in 1886. *Courtesy of Sharpsteen Museum.*

or tea much like they did with liquor. As places to sip hot drinks, coffee saloons were very popular; as replacements for inebriation, not so much. Since the Nielsens provided claret alongside tea and coffee, they clearly did not adhere to the temperance part of the coffee saloon mentality. In fact, they were one of the only upvalley restaurants or hotels to offer tea, coffee or claret gratis to their customers.

In 1893, the Nielsens closed the St. Helena Restaurant. They may have taken a brief break to try their hands at farming, but by early 1894, they had opened a new restaurant, Nielsen's, on Main Street. As before, they offered "First-class Meals at All Hours" and oysters shipped frozen from the Berwick Bay Fish and Oyster Company in Louisiana and served any style. Nielsen's Restaurant was known as an "excellent place [where] he has done a splendid business, the result of setting a good table and treating his patrons with uniform courtesy."

In the spring of 1895, John Nielsen, in partnership with M.R. Garner, purchased the Grand Hotel in St. Helena. Mrs. Nielsen managed the menu and the kitchen while John oversaw the dining room and Garner the bar and guest rooms. Nielsen and Garner did extensive renovations and updates, but the hotel was a money pit. After only five months, John sold the business, but he never recovered from the financial strain. One morning in February 1896, he took a bottle of his wife's medicinal carbolic acid to his woodshed and drank it. Mrs. Nielsen found his body a few hours later. It was later revealed that he had tried to take his life two months prior with strychnine. John was only forty-four years old.

Stewed Oysters
Recipe reprinted from *The Caterer* by the *Napa Journal*, 1885

Take twenty-five bearded oysters (fresh ones are always better than salt, for they do not shrivel in the cooking), strain them from the liquor, and put them in a bowl and add to them a teaspoonful of lemon juice. Then put the liquor of the oysters together with the beards, into a saucepan, adding a whole mace, four of five peppercorns, a pinch of cayenne pepper, a very little grated nutmeg and a piece of lemonrind [sic] the size of a "nickel."

Place the saucepan over the fire; let the liquor simmer very gently for fifteen minutes; then strain it, and thicken it with a teaspoonful of flour, in which an ounce of butter has been smoothly rubbed. Now add a gill of cream, and stir the liquor over a gentle fire until it becomes thick and smooth. Then put in the oysters and let the pan remain only long enough for them to become heated through. Do not allow them to boil or they will shrivel and become tough. As soon as they are heated, have ready some slices of toast on a hotdish, and over these pour the oysters, with their gravy, and serve immediately.

Scalloped Oysters
Recipe by Sarah D. printed in the *Sacramento Daily Union*, 1877

Have good, light bread, dry enough to crumb nicely; roll between the hands until fine and smooth; then rub in melted butter enough to make it rich; put a thin layer in the baking dish; then a layer of oysters—having drained them—alternate thus until the dish is full, seasoning each layer of oysters; finish with buttered crumbs; now pour on the oyster liquor until you can just see it under the surface; put in a quick oven—bake a rich brown; I think break [sic] preferable to crackers, because it is lighter; crackers will always be more clammy or pasty. The better you make your bread the better and handsomer will be your scalloped oysters. To housekeepers who have only canned oysters in reach, I would say that this treatment makes them resemble the fresh more closely than any I have ever tried.

PART III

ROOM AND BOARD

IN 1850, TWO YEARS AFTER THE EMPIRE SALOON OPENED, Nathan Coombs, Lyman Chapman and Samuel Starr built the American Hotel on Main Street, Napa. It was the first hotel and first regular framed building (basically, a square-ish shape) in Napa County, and spectators came from far and wide to witness the men raise the frame. Coombs treated everyone to a staggering $400 worth of eggnog. In later years, the hotel prided itself on a "Culinary Department…under the charge of accomplished Cooks." Individual meals cost twenty-five cents, the higher price indicating the food was above average, accommodations appealing and service commendable. Sometime between 1853 and 1856, Elijah True built the Soscol House near the ferry crossing at the Napa River. While their stagecoaches were ferried across the river, travelers took a break from their journeys at its bar while locals celebrated with parties and balls. Today, Villa Romano, a classic Italian restaurant, inhabits the building. Both hotels were popular with locals and visitors alike, not only for their comfortable rooms but their enticing menus as well.

Hotels and restaurants that offered lodging typically operated on one of two plans. The European Plan offered rooms and food at separate prices. Meals were either sold as a full meal for a set price or à la carte. The American Plan, on the other hand, charged a flat daily fee covering meals and a room. This was the simpler option, but it also led to a lot of wasted food. Because of the massive number of dishes available, American Plan facilities required a larger staff than European Plan ones. No

The Soscol House when it was the Soscol Antiques and Collector's Mart in the 1970s. When the intersection of Highways 29 and 12 was built, the hotel was moved about five hundred feet west and south to its current location. *Courtesy of Napa County Historical Society.*

A parade in front of the Europa Hotel and Restaurant in Calistoga, proprietor Fortunato Luigi "Louis" Banchero, in the late nineteenth or early twentieth century. *Courtesy of Sharpsteen Museum.*

wonder that over time the European Plan became the standard. On that plan, two separate businesses—the restaurant and the lodging house—operated in conjunction with each other while customers got exactly what and how much food they wanted, simultaneously reducing waste and increasing profits.

There are examples of both plans in Napa. The only two restaurants in Napa city in late 1863 each operated on different plans: the Exchange Restaurant on the American Plan and the French Restaurant on the European Plan. The Napa Hotel also had a restaurant (known alternately as the Napa Restaurant, Napa City Restaurant and Napa House Restaurant) that operated on the European Plan. When it opened in 1876, the Magnolia Hotel in Calistoga may have operated on the American Plan.

Chapter 6
Exchange and French Restaurants

In January 1861, F.C. Tuthill opened the Exchange Restaurant across the street from the courthouse on Brown Street. He offered meals at all hours, fresh oysters and seasonal produce. The "ne plus ultra of eating houses," as the *Napa County Reporter* described it, shifted ownership and locations two years later. John S. Hogan merged his restaurant with his recently acquired Napa Hotel, while E. Harry Mower left the Valley House Restaurant, moved into the old Napa Restaurant site and took over the Exchange Restaurant's name.

Mower switched the Exchange to the American Plan but kept the high quality established by Tuthill. Rooms were also available for a daily rate of one dollar and weekly at six dollars. Mower marketed his fifty-cent meals as high class: "Every luxury and all the substantial articles in the provision line…will always be found at this Restaurant. The best of cooking and attendance will combine to please all who may favor the Proprietor with their patronage." Nothing is known of either Mower or Tuthill, and both they and the restaurant vanish from the records after 1863.

The French Restaurant on Main Street, Napa, probably opened sometime in the late 1850s. Despite the name, the French Restaurant did not have an exclusively French menu. Restaurants with "French" or "Paris" in their names were more closely related to Napa County's present-day American-style restaurants like Gillwoods Cafe and the Charter Oak than the haute cuisine of the French Laundry or the Restaurant at Meadowood. Even the presence of a French cook had little effect on the style of food prepared.

French cooks had an aura of respectability that others did not. Since restaurants were French in origin and fine French food was complex and luxurious, French cooks would be highly skilled—or so the theory went.

Not all French restaurants had French cooks and not all French cooks worked at French restaurants. What made Napa County's nineteenth-century French restaurants "French" was the presence of at least one of these things: a French owner or proprietor, a French cook or a few French dishes on the menu. Who established the French Restaurant is currently unknown, but there is a good chance that person was an immigrant from a French-speaking country.

Lucien and Louisa Roux emigrated from France before 1860 and were in Napa in 1861, when Lucien entered into a business partnership with G. Brown. The men took over the French Restaurant from Belgian immigrant Peter Van Bever, who left food service for the grocery business and later the wine industry. With a little remodeling and turning the kitchen over to an experienced French cook, Roux and Brown declared their restaurant "a favorite place of resort for the lovers of good eating." Meals were available anytime and cooked to order. To celebrate Independence Day, Brown and Roux hosted a special dinner feast of turkey, chicken and other fowl, as well as "the Delicacies of the Season."

The French Restaurant was in a good-sized building with five rooms, including private family quarters, public lodging areas, kitchen and dining room. As with many other eateries in the area, it also had beds to let, but because it was on the European Plan, meals cost extra. In a moment of financial cunning, Roux raised the boarding price by a dollar but advertised that he had instead *reduced* the price.

Brown sold out in 1862. Roux kept the place for another few years before clearing out and moving to San Francisco to run a boardinghouse. The French Restaurant was taken over in 1864 by Eugene Eglin, who, like Roux, had been born in France. He and his wife, Catherine, arrived first in New York, where they had their only child, Emma, before relocating to Napa. Eugene made few changes to the French Restaurant. He even kept the same advertisements Roux posted, just swapping out the name of the proprietor. Soon he expanded room and board options to accommodate lodgers by the day, week or month. Poor health forced him to close the French Restaurant in the fall of 1878. Afterward, the Eglins settled in San Francisco, where Eugene opened another restaurant before passing away a few years later.

Chapter 7
Napa Hotel

James Harbin was the first proprietor of the Napa Hotel. He opened it in 1851 but dropped it five years later. The Harbins left for Lake County and there, a few miles from Middletown, established the Harbin Hot Springs resort. Guests could take a boat from San Francisco to Napa, hop on the train up to Calistoga and then catch a specially designated stagecoach at the Magnolia Hotel in Calistoga. Sadly, the resort property was destroyed in the 2015 Valley Fire.

The Napa Hotel changed hands twice after Harbin until John S. Hogan came into the picture in 1862. As a lad, he emigrated from Tipperary, Ireland, to New Orleans before landing in Napa. He worked in Coombs's American Hotel for two years and then went to Healdsburg, where he met and married another Irish immigrant, Ellen. He returned in 1860 and opened the Napa Restaurant on Main Street.

Like most restaurant owners, he offered not just meals but lodging as well. Guests could board by the day (one dollar) or week (six dollars), but the real star was the food. Every morning, hot egg muffins, waffles, cakes with fresh butter and honey were on hand. Oysters, strawberries and cream and "the most delicious ice-cream [*sic*] that ever slipped down a parched throat" were put out for special events. The cook was Harry Moore, who "[presided] over the culinary department, and [knew] exactly how to meet the wishes of the most fastidious."

After renovating the restaurant in 1862, Hogan opened up a separate room for private parties and groups of women. Moore left about the same time, and an unknown cook took his place, but the menu's high quality remained. A hungry dinner guest could feast on soup made from fresh clams or Oregon-raised oysters, baked salmon, trout, ham with new potatoes, beef tongue with turnips, corned beef and cabbage, mutton with caper sauce, roast beef, pork, lamb with green peas, veal with cranberry sauce, pig with currant jelly, turkey with plum jam, chicken and cauliflower, chicken fricassee, veal curry, mutton potpie, carrots, radishes, onions and lettuce. For dessert, they could choose from custard pudding; strawberries and cream; fresh peaches and cream; nuts; almonds; raisins; and apple, custard, cranberry, gooseberry, peach or strawberry pie. They could wash it all down with tea, coffee or chocolate, all for just fifty cents.

Hogan especially liked to go all out for Christmas and Fourth of July. On Christmas Day 1862, he whipped up a meal of "game of varieties to tempt the appetite of a king, and viands, 'done to a turn,' with vegetables, fruit confectionery, pies, puddings and pastry in such abundance that a diner at his table on that day will have exhausted a guest's appetite before he has had a taste of all the good things before him, and all for four bits!—to say nothing of the 'egg-nog.'"

A few days after his Christmas festivities, Hogan took over the lease for the Napa Hotel. This was a big step up for him. The American Plan hotel had rooms for one hundred guests and employed many servants and attendants to provide for the guests' every need. He changed over to the European Plan and offered meals at all hours. After a few months, he bought the hotel outright. Soon Hogan blended together American and European Plans to offer meals at all hours and to people who were not guests. He also added a lodging rate for his rooms so that for six dollars, guests could either take a room and find their own meals or for seven to eight dollars have meals included.

By 1867, Hogan was raking in the cash. He owned the whole block (colloquially known as Hogan's Block) and a bunch of land around the city. That same year, he painted the hotel a gleaming white and updated the interior yet again. He changed the bill of fare regularly depending on what was seasonal and available in the markets. Perch appeared on the menu in May 1871 when he acquired 250 pounds of it that had been hauled out of Tomales Bay. That September, perch was out and "salmon bellies" and "hyperion fritters" were in. Also on the menu were chicken gumbo, oxtail soup, "Italione maccaroni," chicken curry, leg of lamb with mint sauce, ham, corned beef, roast beef, mutton, veal, pork with applesauce, turkey with cranberry sauce, stuffed chicken, venison with strawberry jelly, two kinds of potatoes, cauliflower, turnips, peas, lima beans and butter beans. For dessert there was pie—apple, strawberry, peach and grape—plum pudding with Cognac sauce, seckel pears, grapes, cantaloupe, nuts, raisins and watermelons grown at the nearby Magnolia Farm.

An Italian cook, Angelo Testa, and a French cooking range were installed in 1873, or as the *Napa County Reporter* put it, "The Napa Hotel long famous for the excellence of its *cuisine*, has in the shape of cooking apparatus out Heroded Herod." The following year, Hogan followed through on an earlier vow to replace the wooden building with a brick one. Designed by local architects R.H. Daley and Theodore Eisen, the new building was four stories and had architectural flourishes like pediments, pinnacles, balustrades, a mansard roof and a thirty-one-foot-tall tower. There was also space available for ten other businesses. Between construction and furnishings, "Prince John," as the *Napa County Reporter* dubbed him, spent about $125,000 ensuring his hotel remained the jewel of the city.

Hogan did not get to enjoy his new hotel for very long, for he died in 1877. He was so beloved that the church could not hold all the mourners who attended his funeral, and the procession to Tulocay Cemetery included ninety-nine carriages; hundreds more walked. His widow, Ellen, took over the family business and ran it with the same insistence on high quality.

Things went well under Ellen's guidance until November 1884, when the flames from a lamp caught the building on fire. Guests and employees scrambled out of the windows and out into the streets below. Although the building was brick, the original wooden frame underneath went up like a tinderbox. The speedy response of the fire brigades and easy access to water from the Napa River kept the fire from spreading. The other businesses in the building were saved, but the hotel itself was almost completely destroyed.

A few months later, Ellen rebuilt the hotel. This time, the one-hundred-seat dining room was at the end of the hall past the grand staircase. It was "well lighted and high walled…[and] furnished with new extension tables and chairs; and we may say right here that nothing old or second-handed has gone anywhere into the hotel. New dishes and crockery by the ton, and a handsome array of silverware and glassware are displayed upon the closet shelves."

She also hired a French cook familiar with hotels and supplied the kitchen with the latest equipment. Now there were only two spaces available for stores on the ground floor; the rest was given over to an office and reading room with large plate-glass windows, a bar, a billiard room, a card room

Above: Close-up of the Napa Hotel from E.S. Moore's 1889 illustration of Napa. *Courtesy of Napa County Historical Society.*

Opposite: The Napa Hotel about 1915. *Courtesy of Napa County Historical Society.*

and a sample room for on-the-road salespeople. Twenty-six rooms filled the second floor, as well as a parlor and communal bathrooms. There were twenty-seven more rooms on the third floor. Designed in the Eastlake style by architect Felix Marcuse and built by local contractors and carpenters, the structure had a contemporary and expensive feel.

Ellen stepped away from day-to-day management of the hotel two years later and eventually sold the property. Stricken with pneumonia, she passed away in 1891. After the Hogans, the hotel frequently changed hands. Some were better than others, but none was as diligent as John or Ellen. One manager, Henry Wolf, gave into his racist instincts and fired all Chinese employees in 1892, the height of anti-Chinese sentiment in California. Most had worked in the kitchen or as servers in the dining room.

Room and Board

The restaurant also had its ups and downs. In 1897, a new grill room was installed, and Mrs. Hawley took over the facility. Open until 1:00 a.m., her restaurant featured tamales made by Juana Garcia, salads, oysters any style, ice cream and cake. Christmas dinner in 1898 was as lavish as during the Hogan tenure: eastern oysters, salted peanuts, anchovies on toast, cream of chicken soup, consommé princesse, fillet of sole with tartar sauce, potatoes duchesse, boiled capon with egg sauce, chicken marengo, quails en caisses, pineapple fritters with kirsch, beef ribs en jus, turkey with oyster dressing and cranberry sauce, suckling pig with applesauce, wild duck with currant jelly, turkey with aspic jelly, fresh crab with mayonnaise, mashed and boiled potatoes, celery, pickled walnuts, olives, asparagus with melted butter, Brussels sprouts, new peas, vanilla ice cream, plum pudding with hard and brandy sauce, pies (Boston cream, mince, Charlotte Russe), cakes (fruit, angel), macaroons, dates, figs, fruit and gorgonzola cheese.

By the 1920s, the dining room offered American and Spanish food, either à la carte or table d'hôte (a set menu with a fixed price and no substitutions). Enchiladas were available on weekends. The Napa Delicatessen opened in the Napa Hotel building in 1925 but was unconnected to the hotel's restaurant. Sandwiches, salads, deli meats, pie, ravioli and pre-cooked hot and cold dishes were on hand all day long, even for a sit-down lunch.

Chinese dishes replaced Spanish ones in 1926 with Shanghai Low. On the bill of fare was chow mein, chop suey, egg foo young with crab, chicken fried rice and noodles with roast pork and eggs, and all came with cake and tea. Food from both menus was available late into the evening and for dine-in or take-out. Dinner of an entrée, soup, salad, vegetables, bread and butter, dessert and drinks cost a mere sixty cents. During the day (usually about 11:00 a.m. to 2:00 p.m.), there was the merchant's lunch option, an affordable and quick meal. By the mid-1930s, ethnic foods were out and a buffet and grill were in.

In 1945, the building was listed as a fire hazard by the city after an electrical inspector found the wiring was chaotically installed. Not long after that, the city tore the whole thing down. From 1954 to 1998, the site was home to Brewster's, an army-navy surplus store that also sold camping gear and work clothes. That building was razed as part of the early twenty-first-century downtown revitalization project, and the present building holds assorted shops and eateries.

Chapter 8
Magnolia Hotel (Calistoga)

One spring day in 1866, newlyweds John and Jane Chesebro moved to Napa city. Their journey took them by ship around Cape Horn from Rhode Island, where they were married. This was Jane's first trip west, but John had savings from years spent gold mining in the Sierras. John managed the Revere House for two years and then went up to Sam Brannan's Calistoga Hot Springs for a season. Next he purchased a former dry goods store on the east side of Lincoln Avenue near Washington in Calistoga. He converted it into a saloon and chop house with a "splendid new cooking range…to supply all the hungry, who give him a call, in short order." In 1876, he bought the land next door and erected the grand Magnolia Hotel.

The Magnolia was built to impress. Under its two and a half stories were forty rooms "furnished with the latest and most approved styles of furniture," as well as a billiard room, a bar, bathrooms, a laundry, a wine room, hot sulphur baths, steam baths and a barbershop that was for many years managed by a Black man, J.E. "Nick" Nichols. Visitors stayed for a few weeks to several months, and some even for the full season. Two years after opening, Chesebro built an addition that added two more guest rooms and, in a move that today seems disgusting and environmentally irresponsible but back then was common practice, also installed a sewer line that ran from the hotel straight into the Napa River. Gas lighting was installed in 1889, the mark of a true first-class hotel. Coincidentally, the process by which the gas was produced from gasoline was invented by Edgar Badlam, son of Alexander Badlam, a Mormon pioneer and son-in-law of Calistoga's founder, Sam Brannan.

    Meals were provided to guests as part of the American Plan, but locals had plenty of opportunities to sample the wares. Seemingly every other week there was a dinner, supper, ball or party with tables "loaded down with good things, and every dish gotten up in a manner that did not fail to tickle the palate of those considered good judges." It was the best place in Calistoga to see traveling actors, musicians and other performers. The Magnolia was the town's polling place for elections and played host to meetings of local politicians and fraternal organizations. One supper held by the local chapter of the Order of the Eastern Star, a co-ed branch of the Masons, started at midnight and seated 112 people around two massive tables, each furnished with an "abundance of food, including substantials as well as delicacies."

    John Chesebro died suddenly in 1893, so the hotel passed to his only child, Edward. After a few years, Edward and Jane leased the hotel to Paul Van Loon. After the latter's debts mounted, Edward and Jane's entire inheritance—the hotel, livery, swimming baths, homestead property and their private home on Washington Street—was stripped from them and sold off in a sheriff's auction. Van Loon left to recoup his losses with a new hotel venture in Stockton. The editors of the *Napa Journal* speculated that the root cause of Van Loon and the Chesebro's financial struggles lay in the town's retail liquor license. A few years earlier, Calistoga had increased the license fees to $100 per quarter. Some hoped to increase local revenue while others intended to drive out "bad men and their bad business." While the fee did shutter many saloons, it also took down their beloved Magnolia Hotel, which could neither afford to lose the revenue from the bar by closing it nor pay the $400 yearly retail liquor license fee. An ordinance that cut the quarterly fee in half was drawn up, but it was too little too late for the Chesebros and Van Loon.

    The next owner was Samuel W. Kenyon and his wife, Ella, formerly the proprietors of the Windsor Hotel in St. Helena. In 1900, a year after taking over the Magnolia, Samuel ran for state senator on the Democratic ticket but lost handily to Republican Robert Corlett, a Napan by way of the Isle of Man whose family designed and built many of the historic buildings in Napa city. With his tail between his legs, Kenyon gave up the hotel and left for Ukiah.

    During the late nineteenth and early twentieth centuries, Calistoga suffered repeated fires that devastated the town. The first big one erupted in August 1885 from a room in the Cosmopolitan Hotel and consumed every wood-frame building within reach of the one-hundred-foot flames. Once it hit the liquor store and livery, the added fuel combined with the strong winds blowing through the valley and the lack of a large water supply nearly drove the fire into the Magnolia Hotel. Fortunately, the hotel was spared, but Chesebro's barn and numerous other buildings on Lincoln Avenue were lost in the conflagration.

Another small fire broke out in 1889 on the roof of the Magnolia Hotel, but because Jane spotted it early enough, it was extinguished before it caused too much damage. The hotel's luck held for the 1890 fire that broke out a few doors down. The American Hotel, a livery and several stores and saloons were reduced to ashes. This time there was no wind and plenty of water (some of which was supplied by Chesebro himself), so by the time the flames reached the Magnolia, firefighters were able to defend it. A fourth fire broke out in 1892, again on the hotel's roof. Like the last time, it was quickly put out.

The fifth fire in 1901 was one too many for the Magnolia. On a blisteringly hot day in August, a fire broke out in a store on Lincoln Avenue and raced through the Spiers livery (the same livery that suffered in the 1885 and 1890

The Calistoga Hotel and Groenweld's Restaurant sometime after 1905. *Courtesy of Sharpsteen Museum.*

fires). Firefighters were stymied by the heat, high winds, little water and a hose being burned, and so the flames torched both sides of the streets. Within two hours, most of the downtown business district and several homes were lost, including the Magnolia Hotel. Guests at the hotel sought refuge in the homes of generous locals.

New owners constructed a new hotel, the Calistoga, over the ashes of the Magnolia in 1902. Later developers chopped off the veranda and the entire second and third floors and the first-floor porticoes, but the replacement building still stands at 1422–30 Lincoln Avenue.

Chapter 9
Aetna Springs Resort

As with most important sites, the story of Aetna Springs Resort is fraught and compelling. From cinnabar mine to rustic getaway to idle playground for the rich and famous to a tax haven for a religious group to ruins, this old Pope Valley locale has seen it all.

Before the resort, there was the Valley Mining Company, founded in 1867. For nearly a decade, laborers, most of whom were Chinese, blasted, picked and dug cinnabar out of the hillsides. The work was arduous and dangerous, and cinnabar, once processed into quicksilver (also called mercury), was highly toxic. Quicksilver was a vital component in processing gold. California cinnabar mines, several of which were in Napa County, produced half the world's supply from the 1850s through the 1890s, after which quicksilver was replaced with cyanide.

By the late 1870s, the mining camp was abandoned. Chancellor Hartson, a Napan who had the triple distinction of being wealthy, well respected and virulently anti-Chinese, purchased the land in 1877. He set up a water company to take advantage of the two hot and two soda springs, as well as a small resort for tourists to take the waters. William Lidell took over shortly thereafter. He added a summer house, a store, a laundry, a pavilion with a dance floor, a swimming pool, two bathhouses, a reading room and library, several single and double guest cottages, a dining room and a kitchen. The old stone wall that still runs about a mile along the property line was built by Chinese laborers; given Hartson's repugnant opinions of the Chinese, they may have been hired by Lidell.

Len D. Owens purchased the site in the late 1880s after a visit to the springs supposedly cured his terminal illness. When he opened the golf course in 1894, Len had little idea it would become one of the oldest golf courses in the West. It survived for the next 124 years, through feast and famine. He also hired famous Bay Area architect and old college pal Bernard Maybeck to design a large dining hall, social hall and clubhouse. Maybeck designed numerous structures across the country but is perhaps most known for the ornate Palace of Fine Arts in San Francisco. His redwood dining hall at Aetna Springs featured two rooms, a main seating area and a smaller side room. With its "laminated trusses" and "curved arches," the interior had a "cathedral-like affect [sic]." The secondary room was for guests with restrictive or special diets and was later used for extra seating and as a children's dining area.

The menu at Aetna Springs was just as fancy as the resort itself. One dinner in July 1904 consisted of braised calf's heart, pineapple fritters au jus, prime rib, spring lamb with mint jelly, steamed and mashed potatoes, string

The balcony often hosted a band of musicians to entertain the guests. *Courtesy of Napa County Historical Society.*

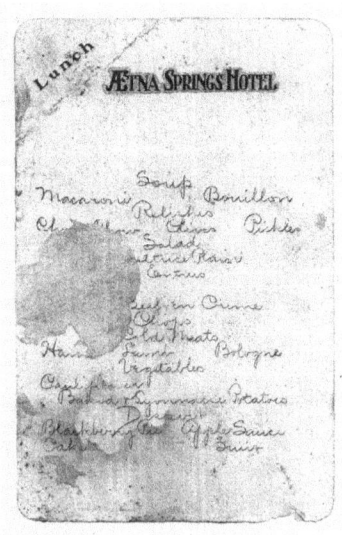

An undated lunch menu of "macaroni soup," bouillon, salad, beef, ham and bologna, vegetables, boiled potatoes, blackberry pie, applesauce, cake and fruit. *Courtesy of Napa County Historical Society.*

beans, summer squash and a cheese plate. On the property were a large orchard, vegetable garden and vineyard to supply the kitchen with fresh produce and table wine. Len built a second clubhouse in 1909 with a long buffet table and a grill for guests feeling peckish after the dining hall was closed. During Prohibition, the resort hired a Chinese chef named Pon Ton. He hired several of his compatriots to work in his kitchen as assistant cook, fry cook and baker, as well as in the pantry and as dishwashers.

As a side note, one of Len's daughters was Marion Benson Owens, known by her stage name Frances Marion, a screenwriter in the early days of Hollywood. She wrote more than three hundred stories and scenarios and directed two movies during her long film career. Frances also wrote a novel called *Valley People* that was supposedly inspired by Pope Valley. Although the characters were probably not based on real people, some locals took affront to her exposing their isolated little valley in such a public way.

Len lived at Aetna Springs until his death in 1945. The year before, George Heibel bought the resort and brought his whole family up there to live. When describing to anthropologist Dr. Felicia Shinnamon his childhood summers spent at Heibel's resort, Dr. Richard Lyons recalled:

> *The dining hall was really immaculate, with beautiful redwood and high ceilings. The food was absolutely excellent and we had a glorious time. We all dressed up to have meals in the dining hall. The barbecues were great too....A typical day at Aetna began with waking up in the screened in bungalow, having buffet breakfast together, and then going over to the barn to saddle up the horses and teach the kids to ride....Later we would all take a swim and have a buffet lunch....In the evenings we would have cocktails at one of the family's bungalows before a delicious dinner.*

On the steps of Aetna Springs' dining hall, an actor named Ronald Reagan announced his candidacy for governor of California in 1966. They celebrated with a barbecue. *Courtesy of Napa County Historical Society.*

As the decades ticked by, the Heibels came to the painful realization that the resort industry was dying. People were no longer interested in spending the summer at a rural retreat. George closed the resort in 1972 and sold the property. After ninety-five years, the resort was dead.

Two failed attempts to build condos on the property later, the mysterious New Education Development Systems bought the site. Soon enough, the true owners were revealed to be the Unification Church of the United States, a religion founded by Korean missionary Sun Myung Moon. Controversy erupted in Napa County as government officials and locals clashed with the group over permits and usage. Meanwhile, the historic buildings fell into disrepair through neglect and disuse.

New owners took over in 2003, and much of the last two decades has been spent trying and failing to kickstart renovation projects. The latest developer as of December 2018 wants to "restore the historic property to its original grandeur through the development of a world-class luxury resort that showcases Napa's food and wine combined with leading wellness programs." Whether or not that dream will come to pass is still up in the air. In the meantime, there will always be fond memories of barbecues and formal dinners in a distant valley.

Mutton Chops
Recipe printed in the *Independent Calistogian*, 1880

The best way to dress mutton chops is to grill them on a gridiron, and when transferred to a hot water-plate or dish, put a piece of butter of the size of an acorn on each, and pepper them. For potato-chips, peel fine kidney-potatoes, cut them in very thin round slices, lay them in a cloth to dry, and fry in the wire basket in good fat; clarified pot-skimmings are preferable to dripping, and beef-suet melted down with lard is next best, but oil is the best of all for frying potatoes. The chips should be sufficient only to cover the bottom of the basket. When taken out they should be laid on paper before the fire, that the grease may be absorbed.

Fillet of Veal, to Stuff
Recipe printed in the *Napa Journal*, 1892

Take a slice or two of the fillit [sic] and a few slices of pork, chop very fine. Add sweet herbs, pepper and salt, moisten with eggs.

PART IV

CHILI QUEENS AND TAMALE MEN

The Wappo and Southern Patwin arrived in the Napa Valley approximately four thousand to ten thousand years ago. With its fertile soil and temperate climate, food sources were abundant. They dined on fish, shellfish and waterfowl from the rivers and creeks. In the woods and meadows, they hunted deer, fowl, bears and other game large and small. Fruit, berries, roots, bulbs, sweet clover, California hazelnuts, milkweed and honey also made it into their meals, but acorns were the staple. After the community harvest, women processed the nuts by drying, shelling, leaching of tannic acid and grinding with stone mortars and pestles. All manner of foodstuff could be produced from acorn flour.

Like many Native people of Northern California, both the Wappo and Southern Patwin cultivated the landscape through frequent burnings—the Wappo doing it at least yearly. Not only did it clear the land and reduce the risk of severe wildfires, but it also allowed certain edible plants like wild oats, tarweed and other native grasses and seeds to grow. There were even special types of burnings done to flush out grasshoppers, caterpillars and other protein-rich insects. Burning as cultivation was so common that many of the peace treaties signed between the Spanish and Mexican soldiers and Indigenous people in the 1800s included clauses regulating burnings, particularly during droughts.

Mexican soldiers and padres did not tour the Napa region until the 1820s; however, it had been on their radar for years. Mexican soldiers battled the Southern Patwin over control of the southeastern portion of Napa County, and the Wappo on the western side of the county were well aware of the ever-encroaching soldiers and missionaries. Try as they might, they were ultimately unable to stop the incursion. A mission and fort were established in Sonoma County, and by the early 1840s, Napa was carved up into fifteen sprawling land grants.

Forced onto missions and ranchos, the Wappo and Southern Patwin modified their traditional eating habits by adding foodstuffs introduced into the valley by Californios, such as corn, wheat, beans, watermelon, onions, chili peppers, beef, mutton and poultry. But adaptation was not a one-way street. Californios learned from Indigenous people which native plants were edible and how to prepare them. María Juárez, wife of Cayetano Juárez, who owned Rancho Tulucay east of the Napa River near downtown Napa, foraged for local plants like angelica and stinging nettle. She mixed those with rosemary brought over from Europe and cooked alongside the Southern Patwin women who labored on her rancho. Like other Spanish and Mexican colonists, María prepared dishes created by pre-Hispanic Indigenous people in Latin America and modified to Spanish tastes, such as tamales and tacos.

The Juárezes' second adobe, constructed in about 1845, was turned into a restaurant in the mid-twentieth century. When this photo was taken in 1977, it was the Old Adobe Hut. *Courtesy of Napa County Historical Society.*

In the county's early years, most people who ate Mexican food were former Californios or Americans who had lived in the area when it was still Alta California. In Napa city, people of Mexican and/or Indigenous heritage congregated in "Spanishtown" (between Main, Pearl and Vallejo Streets and the railroad tracks), what had been the southern part of Salvador Vallejo's Rancho de Napa. Unfortunately, records of the names, addresses and menus of the early Spanishtown eateries no longer exist, but they likely served a mix of Mexican and American dishes.

Through the 1880s, Napans outside Spanishtown consumed Mexican food generally only on special occasions, such as a ball or banquet. They also indulged in a festival staple called a bull's head breakfast or bull's head barbecue. This lavish feast from Californio tradition is exactly what it sounds like—a roasted and heavily spiced head of a bull served alongside frijoles, chili, tortillas, pollo and other Mexican dishes. Across the Southwest United States, street vendors had been selling cheap Mexican food out of carts, stands and their own homes for years, but it took until the 1890s for the trend to catch on in Napa.

Chapter 10
Tamale Parlors

For many nineteenth-century Americans, Mexican food was considered exotic and a little dangerous. Doctors warned patients against the hazards of spicy foods. Latinas who sold chili from stands in a plaza in San Antonio, Texas, were derided as "chili queens," seductive and coarse women who used sexual appeal to entice strangers to purchase their wares. A Napan with the initials T.D.S. published a disdainful poem in the *Napa Journal* about a woman who was temerarious and romantically picky; because she did not secure a respectable man when she was young, she had to settle for "a peon from Autlan [Autlán de Navarro, a city in Jalisco, Mexico]…A bold tamale man."

Of the people who sold Mexican food, the women were not wanton sirens nor the men uneducated ruffians. But the idea that Mexican food was inherently cheap was not so easily quashed. In Napa County, home cooks and dining parlors cropped up at the tail end of the nineteenth century, but restaurants were few and far between. Tamale vendors were not as prevalent in Napa County as they were in other parts of the country, but they were common enough. Even if a Napan had not personally frequented a tamale parlor or had tamales delivered to their home, the concept was at least familiar.

Local newspapers contain scattered references to pushcarts and door-to-door tamale sellers, but few include specifics. However, there is information on one: George Fimby. Born to parents descended from Californios, he lived in Napa with his wife, Trinidad, and their nine children. Trinidad was one of at least nine children born to a laborer-turned-farmer from Mexico and his Californiana wife who had moved to the Yountville and Capell Valley regions. Nearly everyone in the family worked to make ends meet. The Fimby children worked at a millinery shop, at a tannery and glove factory, at Mare Island Naval Shipyard and as laborers on farms and ranches. George worked for a time as a deputy marshal and at the Napa Woolen Mills while Trinidad took care of the house on Pearl Street. To earn extra money, she made chicken tamales and he delivered them around town six evenings a week.

Grocery stores supplied canned chili con carne, frijoles, tamales and tortillas, but discerning diners knew fresh was always best. Some local cooks went beyond home delivery and sold their tamales in shops, saloons, delicatessens and bakeries. Some of these cooks were Mexican American, while others were working-class Americans and European immigrants.

German-Swiss immigrant John Stuky moved to Napa not long after arriving in the United States in 1890. In 1903, he married Martha Sciligo, the daughter of an Italian-Swiss farmer who had settled in Carneros. For a few years in the early 1900s, he operated a saloon on Brown Street opposite the courthouse. There for a few months in 1908 he hired another Swiss immigrant to cook for him. William Wehrli was so famous for his culinary talents that he earned the moniker "Tamale Bill." Men visiting Stuky's saloon could gorge on chicken tamales for fifteen cents or frijoles and clam chowder for ten cents. For whatever reason, the relationship did not last. Tamale Bill moved on to Fort Bragg and operated a few tamale parlors. In January 1909, he died by suicide after jumping out of a second-story window.

Two stores on Brown Street—Hunter's Fruit Depot and Godwin Brothers Grocery—sold tamales made by two different cooks, Kapp and Street and Juana Garcia. Kapp and Street are unknown entities; Juana Garcia is not. She did more than sell just to local grocers. In 1897, her tamales appeared on the menu of the Napa Cafe alongside oysters, oyster cocktails, ice cream, cake and other short orders. Her tamales were also featured at the short-lived Spanish-American Chop House, run by her daughter's Mexican American husband, Peter Feliz. And she sold out of her home on Stewart Street (now called Clinton Street) that she shared with her husband, Ruperto, and their children. In 1902, Ruperto and Juana opened Delmonico Spanish Chop House, where they offered oysters and tamales, among other dishes. The chop house did not last long, and by 1904, it had been replaced by the Chicago Meat Market butcher shop.

Undated photograph of George Fimby as a young man. *Courtesy of Napa County Historical Society.*

According to census records, both Juana and Ruperto were originally from Mexico; Ruperto immigrated to the United States in 1850. He brought his wife and her two children by a previous marriage over in 1865, five years after they were married. Once in California, they had three more children. It appears the Garcias never opened another restaurant, but they remained part of the fabric of Napa's Mexican community.

Manull Silkes was born on Samos, a Greek island not far from Turkey. After immigrating in 1910, Manuel, as he was known in the States, made his way to the North Bay. He married Anastacia "Annie" Higuera, and by 1923, they and their children had relocated to Napa. Manuel opened a tamale parlor out of their single-story home at 1020 Vallejo Street. The recipes and most of the cooking were probably handled by Annie. She was a descendant of Nicolás Higuera, the owner of Ranchos Rincón de los Carneros and Entré Napa.

Within a few months, the Silkeses had relocated the parlor to 1143 Main Street (today the parking lot on Main near Pearl Street) and given the business a formal name: Imperial Tamale Parlor. They likely resided on the second floor. The ground floor was dedicated to the restaurant and kitchen, where they produced homemade beef and chicken tamales, enchiladas and other Mexican dishes. In 1926, Annie took full ownership of the parlor, perhaps in preparation for filing for divorce in 1927. A year later, she won full custody of their children. Manuel left Napa but continued to work as a cook in restaurants throughout California. He finally settled in San Joaquin County and stayed there the rest of his days.

Freed from an unpleasant marriage, Annie kept up the Imperial Tamale Parlor. About the same time as she was ditching Manuel, a painter at Mare Island named Walter Olds lost his wife, Laura, to a brief illness. Who knows how the widower and divorcée met, but the two did not stay single for very long. Almost a year to the day after her divorce, Annie and Walter got hitched in Reno, Nevada. He moved in and helped her run the restaurant until about 1930, when they sold the joint and later moved to Vallejo. Walter died in 1949; Annie survived him another four decades and never remarried.

Chapter 11
Dabner Brothers Restaurant

A few doors down from the Imperial Tamale Parlor, brothers Frank and Manuel Dabner opened a restaurant in 1900. Their father, João Pimental Davina, had emigrated from the Azores, Portugal, in the 1840s to Massachusetts, where he Americanized his name to John Dabner. There he met fellow Azorean Maria de Jesus Machado. John mined during the gold rush and earned enough to marry Maria in 1857. Soon they moved their growing family from New Bedford to California, where the brothers were born. The Dabners were fairly influential in San Leandro. Maria started the Holy Ghost Festival in about 1870, which celebrated the Pentecost and honored Queen Isabel of Portugal. After their move to Sonoma County, the Dabners founded another Holy Ghost Festival in 1891.

Frank and Manuel came to Napa County to make a name for themselves. In the 1890s, they ran a grocery store together while Manuel also maintained a farm. Regrettably, they were unsuccessful and declared insolvency in 1898, meaning they were unable to pay their mounting debts. Two years later, they rebranded with a restaurant. Food service ran in their family. Their father's parents ran a bakery on Ilha do Pico, Portugal, and their father had been a cook on a whaling ship.

The dining room of their restaurant was "thoroughly renovated and newly [wall-] papered and painted. Kitchen bright and clean. All the furniture new and also the cutlery and plate ware. Neat and handsome apartments for private parties." The menu was the real draw. Besides the usual American-style fare, they also featured a variety of Mexican dishes:

The bill of fare includes the following with tea or coffee: Porterhouse Steak, 40c; Sirloin, 35c; Beefsteak any style, 25c; Lamb or Pork Chops (3), Mutton Chops, Ham or Bacon, Hamburger Steak or Pork and Beans, 15c. Two Eggs any style, 20c; 3, 25c; [illegible] *Fritters (2), 15c; (3), 25c. Oyster Cocktail and crackers, 10c. Sandwiches, 10c.*

Our specialties: Potted Chicken, with bread, butter and salad, 10c; Chicken or Turkey Tamales, boneless, 15c; Chicken or Turkey Tamales, plain, 10c; Beef Tamales and potato salad, 10c; Chili Con Carne and potato salad, 10c; Mexican Frijoles and potato salad, 10c; Shrimp and Crab Salad, 10c; Frankfort [sausage] *with potato salad, 10c.*

Enchiladas, with bread and butter, 15c; Chorizo Con Huevo, with bread and butter, 15c; Chili Verde Con Queso, with bread and butter, 15c; Albondigas [meatball soup]*, with bread and butter, 10c; Empanadas Fritas, 10c; Croquettes, 10c; Milk, Tea, Coffee or Chocolate, 5c.*

Wine or other liquors served in place of tea or coffee if desired.

Frank and Manuel kept the restaurant open all night, but even with the varied menu, reasonable prices and long hours, the venture folded. By 1904, the brothers were out and Golden State Creamery was in. The restaurant was built practically on top of Napa Creek, making it the perfect spot for a facility that needed to keep its products constantly cool. Frank left Napa soon after, and Manuel followed after 1910. Both died in the early 1920s.

Chapter 12

Spanish Restaurant

Sensing Napans' increasing interest in Mexican food, Edward Quijada (also spelled Quijado) opened his restaurant in 1898. Quijada was born in Napa in the early 1870s to parents who had emigrated from Mexico in the 1850s. Several of his many siblings married into Napa's Mexican American and Californio families, including Inez Carrvajal, who sold homemade tamales out of her home on Stewart Street in 1898. About the same time Quijada opened his restaurant, he married Carlota Hernandez, known to everyone as Lottie, and took in her daughter Caroline.

Edward whipped up the usual assortment of American and Mexican dishes: fifteen-cent beef or chicken tamales, frijoles, enchiladas, roast chicken, salads, eggs, potatoes, steak, bread and butter, coffee, oysters, oyster loaf (a sandwich of fried oysters, possibly invented in San Francisco during the gold rush), chili con carne, chops and short orders. The Spanish Restaurant frequently hosted banquets and dinners for clubs, civic groups, fraternal organizations and local movers and shakers. So many people dined at his restaurant that a *Napa Register* gossip columnist claimed that Edward sold at least eight thousand tamales every month. That might have been intended as a joke, but given how popular his restaurant was, it is quite possible business was that brisk.

Diners at the Spanish Restaurant were greeted by Lottie and served by the ever-cheerful Miguel "Mike" Espinosa. Born in Napa in 1882, Mike was another descendant of prominent Californio families. His maternal grandmother was Sinforosa Juárez, the second-eldest daughter of

Cayetano Juárez. Before waiting tables for the Quijadas, Mike milked and herded cows at Malone Dairy, and after he worked for Riverside Grocery. But music was his passion. As a young man, he was known to practice his violin out in open fields, much to the delight of passersby. Despite his talents, he rarely performed locally, preferring to play with the East Bay Symphony in Oakland.

In 1910, Edward purchased a four-passenger Overland car and worked on the side as a chauffeur. By the 1920s, his financial success was such that he was able to purchase several pieces of downtown real estate to rent out. Finally, Edward retired in 1935. He intended to spend his golden years traveling with his wife and relaxing, but she died suddenly from a heart attack two years later. Edward suffered a stroke in January 1956 that claimed his life. He was eighty-three years old.

Anyone with an enterprise as long-running and well-known as the Spanish Restaurant is bound to attract the odd scandal here and there. For Edward, there was one so famous it became a local legend. Saloonkeeper Charles Reams invited carpenter Sam Boyd to dine at the then three-year-old restaurant. Boyd warned Reams of his huge appetite, but Reams insisted. He then watched Boyd pack away "three dozen fried eggs, a family porterhouse steak, a plate of bread and butter, some potatoes, a cup of coffee, and a bottle of beer." Reams was out three dollars, or about ninety dollars today. Eight months later, Boyd again put his incredible stomach to the test at the Spanish Restaurant. A small but horrified crowd watched as he "would bite off a piece of a goblet, chew it up with a piece of bread, wash it down with a drink of coffee, and apparently seemed to relish it as he would a porterhouse steak."

A few years earlier, an unidentified man was reported to have hustled another unnamed man into buying his dinner, during which he inhaled "five beefsteaks, 16 eggs, 10 biscuits, 4 dishes of potatoes, 3 dishes of sauce, 5 cups of coffee, 3 plates of butter and a generous slice of cake." Could this have been Boyd? Possibly. By that point, he and his family had been in the county for sixteen years. Despite what his gastronomic feats might imply, Boyd lived a long life and died in 1926 after raising eleven children, twenty-four grandchildren and ten great-grandchildren.

The Spanish Restaurant also survived several local and federal alcohol bans. Prohibition hit the county hard when it went into effect in January 1920. Wineries, saloons, boardinghouses, stores, government officials and private citizens argued over the pros and cons, hid secret stashes and ratted each other out. In the early 1900s, Napa city passed several precursors to the Big One. As of 1908, liquor was illegal to sell in restaurants, but the ordinance was violated so regularly that city council briefly debated whether to strike it entirely. They could not come to a consensus but did grant Edward Quijada his petition to offer wine and beer for free with every meal.

To curb prostitution, the city passed an ordinance in 1913 restricting the amount of liquor allowed in rooming houses (what the women who ran brothels called their bases of operation to get around prostitution bans). Four years later, the city again focused on alcohol consumption. This time, the ordinance restricted who could apply for a liquor license, required an extensive list of documents included with the application and designated what activities could and could not take place at the same place liquor was consumed. For example, all applicants had to be U.S. citizens and residents of Napa city. A saloonkeeper could only have instrumental music—no dancing. A hotel wanting a liquor license had to note on its application "the hours at which regular meals are served, and during which beer or wines will be furnished, served, sold or given away."

Oddly, there was one exception for restaurants applying for a license: those "serving tamales, chili-con-carne [sic], or enchiladas to guests thereof, may serve with each tamale, enchilada, or serving of chili-con-carne sold and consumed, a pint bottle of beer or wine." Who made the decision to exempt tamale parlors and Mexican restaurants and why? We may never know, but it certainly is fascinating.

Chapter 13
El Faro Restaurant

While on a much-needed getaway, Gregorio Hernandez "accidentally discovered" Calistoga. Its rustic charm, welcoming hospitality and entertaining amenities were too enticing to pass up. After bringing his wife, Carmen, up to visit, she, too, fell in love with the little town. They closed their Mexican restaurant El Faro in Sunnyvale and moved the business north. In June 1971, they opened a new El Faro Restaurant on Lincoln Avenue.

El Faro offered the usual fare of homemade tamales, chiles rellenos, enchiladas, flautas, tacos, frijoles, tostados, burritos, gallina en salsa, chile colorado and salads, as well as the "Acapulco Surprise" house special. In 1974, they even developed a recipe for vegetarian tacos. Hot sauce and green peppers were served on the side so diners could make the food as spicy as their taste buds could handle.

For Christmas, Carmen decorated one of the windows of El Faro with a scene from the Bible for a contest hosted by a local church. Greg got involved in the local community through his work in the chamber of commerce. For a few years, he also wrote a Spanish-language column, "Lo Que Pasa En Casa," for the *Calistogan*, to which Carmen typically contributed a poem of her own devising. The column briefly discussed local happenings that impacted the county's Mexican and Mexican American population. And, of course, they advertised their restaurant. At home, the Hernandezes raised sheep and entered their dog Fischer Streak Bingo in dog shows.

CHILI QUEENS AND TAMALE MEN

Above: The El Faro Restaurant is in the background, *top center*, in this 1972 photograph of a parade of cars during the Napa County Fair. *Courtesy of Napa County Historical Society.*

Left: A matchbook from the El Faro. *Courtesy of Todd L. Shulman.*

In 1978, El Faro moved a few doors down into the old Reeder's Calistoga Maid Creamery and Restaurant building. The food was just as good as before, leading the *Calistogan* to write: "When the owner here decided to open, he had one primary goal in mind…to offer the people of this area the finest food, served among friendly people in a pleasant atmosphere and always with the best service in town. The fact that he has achieved just exactly that is evidenced by the ever-returning number of people that has made the El Faro Restaurant their place to dine." Greg and Carmen remodeled in the winter of 1982 and added an outdoor patio. Finally, after nineteen years in business, Greg and Carmen closed El Faro in 1987. Seven years later, they bid farewell to Calistoga and moved to Milpitas.

From the late nineteenth through the early twentieth centuries, Mexican food was one of the most popular types of food in Napa. Tastes changed, but Napa never lost its love for chili and tamales. Mexican eateries have maintained a strong foothold in the county, especially as new Latinx immigrants began to arrive in large numbers in the mid-twentieth century. Even tiny townships like Oakville were graced with a good place to nosh on chiles rellenos and tostados with El Cafe Talpita, which opened in 1963. Compadres Rio Grille, first in Yountville and then Napa, was a local favorite for thirty-two years before rising rent prices and labor costs forced it to close in 2019.

When Tacos Chavez hit the streets in the early 1970s, it made history as the first taco truck in Napa County, and it still operates to this day. In a way, taco trucks merely modernized a sales technique that nineteenth-century tamale vendors had perfected: bring the food to the people and make it affordable and at least somewhat authentic. History often repeats itself, but sometimes that repetition can be very tasty indeed.

Chili Sauce
Recipe printed in the *Napa Journal*, 1917

Eight quarts of ripe tomatoes, three cups of peppers, two cups of onions, three cupfuls of sugar, one cupful of salt, one and a half quarts of vinegar, three teaspoonsfuls of cloves and same quantity of cinnamon, two teaspoonfuls each of ginger and nutmeg. Boil three hours. Chop tomatoes, peppers and onions very fine. Bottle and seal.

Stuffed Pasilla Chiles
Recipe provided by Chef Miguel Franco of La Placita
to the *Napa Register*, 1989

4 roasted pasilla chiles
1 clove garlic, finely chopped
1/8 lb. crumbled goat cheese
1/8 lb. grated jack cheese
1 tablespoon shallots, finely chopped
1 1/2 diced sun-dried tomatoes
1/8 cup cilantro, finely chopped
1/8 cup fresh basil, finely chopped
1/4 teaspoon thyme
1 egg
2 tablespoons heavy cream
1/8 cup of light oil
Blue corn meal
Salt and pepper to taste

Roast the chiles and peel them, split open enough to remove the seeds. Combine the remaining ingredients in a bowl. Mix well and shape into rolls or balls that will fit well into the chiles. Stuff the chiles with the mixture and dip them into the egg and cream mixture. Roll the chiles in blue corn meal and fry them in the oil until lightly browned and cheese mixture has melted. Drain well on paper towels and serve a finely diced tomato salsa as an accompaniment. A wedge of lime squeezed over the chile also imparts added zest.

PART V

CHOW CHOP SUEY

THE HISTORY OF THE CHINESE IN CALIFORNIA IS LONG, COMPLICATED and challenging. It is the story of people driven to make a better life for themselves in a country that went out of its way to make that life as difficult as possible. Whether by working as cooks and waiters in homes and hotels or by running their own restaurants, food was a crucial element in helping Chinese immigrants both retain their traditional practices and introduce new experiences into American society.

For decades after the first Chinese restaurant opened—the Canton Restaurant in San Francisco, 1849—they struggled to gain traction with Americans. Many of these early restaurants were simple and tidy affairs operated by well-funded entrepreneurs, with trained staff and experienced cooks serving reasonably priced meals. But restaurateurs fought an uphill battle against racism and stereotypes, fake accusations of filthy dining and cooking conditions and false rumors of the use of rat and dog meat. Eventually, Chinese cooks modified their plates to appeal to American palates and American diners learned to appreciate and indulge in "foreign" foods. Today, there are more than forty thousand Chinese restaurants across the country—more than every Burger King, McDonald's and KFC franchise combined.

The first Chinese immigrants arrived in Napa County in the early 1850s and established Chinatown on the east bank of the Napa River by First Street. Soon, Chinese encampments and towns sprang up across the county, from the mines in the north to the farms in the south and the vineyards in between.

Lost Restaurants of Napa Valley and Their Recipes

A collage made by H.A. Darms of photos of Napa's Chinatown in 1906. Bing Kee's store is top right. *Courtesy of Napa County Historical Society.*

During harvest season, hundreds of Cantonese people, mostly men, packed into these communities as migrant agricultural laborers. There were also many families and workers who lived year-round in Chinatowns in Napa, St. Helena, Calistoga and Rutherford. Some residents liaised with white American employers to bring in laborers from other parts of the state, while others catered to other Cantonese immigrants. There were men who worked in the tanneries and women who worked in laundries, gardeners who grew foods from the old country, doctors who treated ailments with traditional medicines and practices and, of course, restaurateurs who offered a little taste of home.

Chapter 14
Lai Hing Company

While specifics about Chinese-owned businesses that operated in Napa County's Chinese communities are hard to come by, there is some information. An 1889 article in the *Napa Register* wrote about one restaurant in Napa's Chinatown that was next door to a gambling hall and temple. Although the racist terminology does the reporter no favors, this is also one of the only descriptions of an early Chinese restaurant in Napa: "The Chinese restaurant is a place of interest. The heathen are called to their meals, cooked in two large kettles over a brick furnace, by the banging together of cymbals. A large and small table occupy the dining room and the patrons of the restaurant sit on stools and boxes."

Chinese food, made with imported and locally grown ingredients, was also available in boardinghouses. These facilities provided a wide range of different meals. Of the early Chinese-run dining facilities in Napa County, the one we have the most detail on belonged to the Chan family.

Chan Wah Jack arrived in Napa in 1860 to work in the Sang Lung store run by his older brothers Chan Kee Toy, Ah Long and Big Jim. Chan Wah Jack and his second wife, Kin Lim, left with their children to raise them in China, and they all returned to Napa in 1893. After a devastating fire in the Napa Chinatown 1902, the family picked up the pieces and purchased Kay Toy's Lai Hing Company. Besides selling goods from China, the Chans also sold medicinal herbs, provided banking services, let out rooms for lodgers and ran a restaurant.

The Lai Hing Company building fell into disrepair in the 1960s and was torn down in 1967. *Courtesy of Napa County Historical Society.*

When meals were ready, Kin Lim rang a bell, summoning her family and their five to twelve boarders to gather around the dining table. During Lunar New Year, she whipped up a traditional feast for family and friends. According to her son Shuck, her menu included traditional Cantonese "dishes like Tung Gwa Chung (steamed whole winter melon), bok Chit Gai (steamed whole chicken), Fou Opp (roast duck, Cantonese style), Hoi Tom, Bow Yee (seasoned cucumber and abalone), Jing Lo Yee (steamed whole stripped [*sic*] bass)…Jing Horn Yee (steamed pork with salted fish)."

Shuck often provided the meat for his mother's meals, usually fish caught in the Napa River or roasted duck or pig. Roasting a pig was an exhausting

An old cabinet of Chinese medicinal herbs from inside Lai Hing, 1967. *Courtesy of Napa County Historical Society.*

process that required training from an expert. After butchering the pig, it was lowered into an underground brick stove through a system of pulleys and ropes. When fully cooked, the pig was hung up in front of Lai Hing, its meat sliced off on-demand for each customer. Shuck roasted a pig every day—two on weekends—and got so good at it that a man from Sacramento came down specifically to have Shuck train him in the art.

When he was out on his own, Shuck took all the cooking skills he learned from his mother and opened and worked in restaurants in San Francisco; Worcester, Massachusetts; Portland, Maine; and Bangkok. Although traveling the world was quite the adventure for a young, single man, Shuck

Above: Undated photograph of Lee Kum and Shuck Chan wearing traditional Chinese clothing. *Courtesy of Napa County Historical Society*.

Left: Menu from the Shuck Chan Restaurant in Placerville. On the cover is Shuck and Kum's daughter Poy Chan after 1956, when she became the first Chinese American to win the Highway 50 Queen pageant. *Courtesy of Napa County Historical Society*.

longed for the pleasant climate and security of his family back home. He returned to Napa in the 1920s to help his mother run Lai Hing, which soon had more white customers than Cantonese.

Not until 1955 did he finally get back into the restaurant business. By that point he and his wife, Lee Kum, had been married for twenty-five years and had six children. They had watched the city raze Chinatown under the pretense of beautifying the area for a yacht club that was never built, and they relocated Lai Hing into a new building farther up East First Street. Seeking new opportunities, the Chans moved to Placerville. For the next twelve years, they ran a Chinese restaurant that featured decorations like an old wooden wheelbarrow used by Chinese miners from the area. Shuck and Lee eventually returned to Napa and dedicated the rest of their lives to preserving and promoting Chinese history in California.

Chapter 15
Sang Wo's Lunch Counter

Between anti-Chinese sentiment; the shift in labor trends; and rampant exclusion laws, ordinances and state constitutional amendments, Chinese immigration slowed in the early twentieth century. By the time Sang Wo opened his eatery in the 1910s, the Chinese population of Napa County had dropped precipitously.

Sang's restaurant was in a small building behind a saloon called the Russ House at 8 and 10 Brown Street (formerly known as the German House), located on what is now the pedestrian walkway side of the county office building at 1127 First Street. Before Sang, F.W. Walters opened the German Grill in the Russ House in 1909, featuring short orders and an exclusively white staff. He added to the menu oysters prepared in any style and clams fried, stewed and in chowder. Within a few months, Walters was out and longtime business partners Charles Reams and William Chappell were in. They had traded Vallejo for Napa in 1907 when their saloon was shuttered when Vallejo City Council reduced operating licenses by nearly 40 percent at the behest of the U.S. Navy at Mare Island. Every day from 5:00 a.m. to 1:00 a.m., the Russ House served "the best meal for your money." After Reams's death in 1914, Louis Gstrein and Benjamin Green took over the saloon and lodging house. In May 1915, Sang Wo opened his eatery.

Although there are no biographical details on Sang Wo and his restaurant only lasted a short while, it represents an interesting period in American food history. The restaurant bridged the gap between the old and new. He

Reams and Chappell are two of the men standing in front of the German House saloon in this 1906 photo by H.A. Darms. *Courtesy of Napa County Historical Society.*

offered trendy Chinese dishes like chop suey and chow mein, but instead of just tables and chairs like a typical chop suey joint, his place was a lunch counter. Lunch counters had been around since the 1850s. They were cheap and casual places where customers sat on bar stools at a long counter, often facing the kitchen, which could be seen through a large passthrough. Short orders were served alongside more complicated Chinese meals. The short order was the precursor to modern-day fast food, but at the time most short-order meals were typical American-style diner food.

Interestingly, Sang operated a lunch counter even as he maintained the going-out-of-style tradition of serving dinner at noon. Historically, dinner was the main meal of the day and was often eaten between noon and 2:00 p.m. In the evening, people had supper, a light meal designed to tide a person over until morning. As the middle class expanded and more people entered the white-collar workforce in the early 1900s, dinner was pushed back into the evening and lunch moved into the afternoon slot. Dinner, as opposed to lunch, was always hot, while lunch could be hot or cold. By describing his lunch counter as serving dinner at noon, Sang

The layout of a lunch counter in 1955, when this photo of the Silverado Creamery in Calistoga was taken, was not that different from one in 1915. *Courtesy of Sharpsteen Museum.*

distinguished between offering quick bites anytime and full meals in the middle of the day. It was not a trendy description for 1915, but it got his point across.

By 1916, Sang Wo was out of the Russ House and Green and Gstrein reopened their grill. About 1921, the former proprietor of the Owl Restaurant at Main and Third Streets, Herman Peterman, took over the Russ House and grill. As an exciting historical footnote, Peterman was arrested in 1921 for "conducting a place of nuisance, contrary to the Volstead Act, to-wit, having in his possession intoxicating liquors," but after a year of attempting to prosecute him, the case was dropped. P.W. Meyers, the Prohibition agent who had secured the evidence against Peterman, failed repeatedly to appear in court to testify. It was later discovered that he had taken a $10,000 bribe in Santa Rosa and fled the country.

Chapter 16
A-1 Cafe

In the 1930s, Yuen Low, Henry Owyeong, Albert Lee and Ming "Alfred" Wong arrived in Napa from Canton, China. Although they have different surnames, they were actually brothers. The increasingly restrictive series of Asian exclusion acts operating between 1875 and 1965 made it extremely difficult to immigrate to the United States. To get around this, thousands of Chinese immigrants took on "paper names" wherein they acquired documents falsely stating they were related to Chinese American citizens. Not until Chinese immigration laws were loosened in 1943 could paper daughters and sons attempt to get their old names back. For the Wong brothers, only Ming recovered his true surname, while the rest settled for their paper names and passed them down to their children.

According to most sources, the A-1 Cafe opened in 1936. In fact, Vallejo restaurateur Jew Cheong opened it two years earlier. Joining him at the restaurant was Allan Cheong, a relative who worked as a waiter. It was one of only a few Chinese restaurants in town. The Cheongs offered dine-in or take-out of American and Chinese dishes, including chop suey, chow mein, roast chicken and pork, egg foo young and assorted other noodle dishes, as well as wine and beer.

It was chop suey that helped secure Chinese cuisine's place in American society. If asked about the dish's origins, most Americans would probably say it was invented in the United States. One legend holds that it was created in San Francisco during the gold rush by a Chinese cook who tossed leftovers into a wok to serve to several miners who had arrived just as he was about to close. Another roots the origins in an inexperienced cook hired to serve Chinese laborers building the transcontinental railroad who threw a bunch of ingredients together and stir-fried them in hopes the dish would be edible, if not appetizing. A third tall tale claims that when Chinese envoy Li Hongzhang visited New York City, he disliked American-style cooking so much that he took his meals in Chinatown, where he dined on chop suey. All three legends are very likely wrong.

Chow chop suey, as it was originally known, had been on the menu of Chinese eateries in the United States for decades before it became a hot ticket item. Ingredients varied depending on the region in China the cook was from, yet the concept was always the same: animal offal, vegetables and spices stir-fried in a wok and poured, along with the leftover liquid, onto a bowl of rice. The name may be derived from the Cantonese pronunciation of *chao za sui*, a similar dish that cooks brought over on the boat. After Hongzhang's 1896 visit and the subsequent chow chop suey gossip, the dish's popularity skyrocketed.

Unlike the elaborate environments of fancy Chinese restaurants, chop suey joints were simply decorated and more interested in feeding people quickly and efficiently than offering a fine dining experience. Jew Cheong advertised that he had "installed all the latest and most sanitary equipment therein, and he assures all his patrons courteous treatment." Café customers wanted fast, affordable and filling lunches, and Chinese dishes fit the bill perfectly. Women had just begun to enter the business world as typists, secretaries and other sorts of office workers. They sought out chop suey houses in droves, so much so that artist Edward Hopper memorialized that scene in one of his most famous paintings of two women sharing a Chinese meal. Due to its prime downtown location, the A-1 kept extended hours to fill the bellies of Napans for lunch, dinner and after a night on the town: daily from 11:00 a.m. to 1:00 a.m. and Saturdays until 3:00 a.m.

Jew Cheong kept the restaurant until about 1938, when he went back to Vallejo and Yuen Low and his wife, Chan San Yuen (no relations to the Chan Wah Jack family), moved in. Yuen was clever with his ads, effusing them with the highest praise. Under him the restaurant was "the most exclusive Chinese restaurant in Napa," the kind of place where "once you eat here it becomes a habit. You just can't resist the good food!"

Tragically, on December 15, 1944, Yuen was killed in a hit-and-run. After a visit to San Francisco, his car ran out of gas between Rodeo and Hercules in an area known as Oleum (as in "petroleum," named for the Union Oil company town that once existed there). He attempted to cross the highway but was hit by an oncoming car. His family remained in Napa with the restaurant. Alfred Wong worked at the A-1 Cafe as early as 1936 and took over the spot after his brother's death.

Sometime between 1944 and 1947, the restaurant moved a few doors up, from the former site of the Daglia's ravioli parlor in the Napa Hotel Building into the Napa Valley Opera House. Built in 1880 by brothers and architects Samuel and Joseph Newsom, the Italianate-style building was Napa city's premier cultural center for decades. Visitors could hear not only opera but also political speeches, author readings and concert performances. John Philip Sousa's band and San Francisco opera singer Luisa Tetrazzini performed to enthralled Napans; on one occasion, heavyweight boxing camp John L. Sullivan fought an exhibition match on stage. Unlike other opera houses, the stage and seating areas are on the second and third floors while the ground floor is retail and restaurant space.

By the 1950s, the A-1 Cafe was a local favorite. Newspapers in Calistoga and St. Helena wrote rave reviews of the restaurant with "the best Chinese food, the most congenial spirit, and the most clean and attractive of surrounds. People always come back again and again to a place which has built its good name on these standards." Another article applauded the "excellent food cooked by a discriminating chef, wholesomely and deliciously."

The Wongs took over the A-1 Cafe a year before Charles Loring took this photo in 1965. *Courtesy of Napa County Historical Society.*

By the time this photo was taken in the 1970s, the Opera House had been closed for nearly six decades. An owner threatened to demolish the deteriorating building, but it was spared when locals got it in the National Register of Historic Places. *Courtesy of Napa County Historical Society.*

In 1914, competition from the newly opened Empire Theater, with its silent movies and vaudeville performances, proved too much for the Napa Valley Opera House. The owner intended the closure to be brief, yet as of the 1970s it was still shuttered and the building rapidly deteriorating. A decade and several substantial donations later, the opera house was restored to its original glory. However, before improvements could be made, the businesses on the ground floor had to go. In 1982, after forty-eight years in business, the A-1 Cafe closed its doors for the last time.

By that point, Cantonese restaurants were largely being replaced by Mandarin- and Szechuan-style cooking as people from different regions under Chinese influence began immigrating to the United States. In Calistoga, Shan Fan and Mei Ling opened Soo Yuan Restaurant, which served both Mandarin and Szechuan dishes, "much to the delight of the community." A few years later, Taiwanese restaurateur Teng Wei established a Mandarin restaurant in St. Helena and hired another Taiwanese immigrant, Chef Chiang, who was known for being able to cook with three woks simultaneously.

Several men who ran or worked in the A-1 Cafe went on to open restaurants of their own. Albert Lee opened the Golden Dragon restaurant in downtown Napa in 1967, which ran for a few decades. Mama Low's brother David Shui worked at the A-1 with Henry. In the early 1960s, he opened his own restaurant, the China Cafe, three doors up on Main. This was the second China Cafe in Napa city, the first based out of the F. Martin Building on Brown Street in the early 1920s. Bing Hin Yuen, later known as Bing Soon, emigrated from China to California in 1939. He joined the air force during World War II and fought bravely in Germany. For twelve years, from 1947 to 1959, he worked at the A-1 Cafe before opening the Asia Cafe on Main between Second and Third. Although Soon retired in 1987, the restaurant continues to churn out delicious dishes.

Henry Owyeong joined the army in World War II and worked in transport. Afterward, he went to Hong Kong and married Mary Ng before returning to San Francisco in 1949. A decade later, they decided to settle in Napa and take over the family restaurant. Henry and Mary ran the restaurant from 1959 to 1965 before giving it over to Alfred. After that, the Owyeongs opened Wong's House of Chop Suey in the new Bel Aire Plaza in 1965. Where the A-1 featured fast and casual food, Wong's offered a nicer dine-in experience. Their restaurant served "authentic Chinese cuisine" and sold wines produced locally.

Left: The Asia Cafe is the longest-running Chinese restaurant in Napa County history. Photographer Herman Soon, 2019. *Courtesy of Anna and Ping Chu and Herman Soon.*

Right: A matchbook from Wong's House of Chop Suey in Bel Aire Plaza. *Courtesy of Todd L. Shulman.*

Henry had big dreams for Wong's. In 1976, they closed Wong's in Bel Aire to relocate it to a larger, 140-seat, $130,000 brand-new building at 1675 Trancas Street. He took care to give it a "more Chinese atmosphere" by designing the exterior with a steeply pitched and pointed roof and importing interior decorations from China. The name changed from Wong's House of Chop Suey to Wong's Restaurant; however, the hours, prices and friendly service stayed the same, as did the menu, which featured almond chicken, chicken salad and Peking duck. After four decades in the restaurant business, the Owyeongs retired in 1987. Henry died two years later, but Mary lived until 2017.

For nearly forty years, Napa city's Chinese restaurant scene was dominated by Henry Owyeong, Albert Lee and Ming Wong and their descendants and relations. Together, the brothers helped changed the way Napans saw Chinese food. No longer was chop suey something exotic; instead, it became an all-American dish.

Chop Suey
Recipe provided by W.E.S. Fales, former vice consul at Amoy (today called Xiamen), to the *Mariposa Gazette*, 1902

For four persons two chickens' livers, two chickens' gizzards, one pound young, clean pork cut into small pieces, half an ounce of green root ginger and two stalks of celery. Saute this in a frying pan over a hot fire, adding four tablespoonfuls of olive oil, one tablespoonful of vinegar, half a cupful of boiling water, one teaspoonful of Worcestershire sauce, half a teaspoonful of salt, black and red pepper to taste and a dash of cloves and cinnamon. When nearly done, add a small can of mushrooms, half a cupful of either bean sprouts or French green peas or string beans chopped fine or asparagus tips. The see-yu sauce which is eaten with this delectable dish can be procured at any Chinese grocery.

Chop Suey
Recipe printed in the *Napa Register*, 1931

1 ½ to 2 cups shredded cooked lean pork
2 tablespoons fat
1 green pepper shredded
2 cups shredded onion
2 cups shredded celery
Salt to taste
2 cups meat broth or thin gravy
1 teaspoon cornstarch
1 tablespoon cold water
2 cups sliced raw Jerusalem artichokes or radishes
4 tablespoons soy sauce

Brown the meat lightly in half the fat and remove from the skillet. Cook the pepper and onion in the rest of the fat a few minutes. Add the celery, meat, salt, broth or gravy. Cover, and simmer for five minutes.

Mix the cornstarch and water until smooth, stir into the mixture and cook for a few minutes longer. Add the artichokes or radishes, or substitute for them 1 cup of sliced peanuts. Add soy sauce in sufficient quantities to give the desired flavor and then salt to taste.

Serve with hot flaky rice. (This recipe serves 5 persons).

Part VI

Little Italy

Centuries of strife with more powerful European nations and the trials and tribulations of unification, abdications and revolutions pushed thousands of Italians out of their homeland in the late nineteenth and early twentieth centuries. Between 1850 and 1880, those who came to the United States were mostly from northern Italy, and from the 1880s into the 1920s they were generally from the south.

Those who arrived in California had plenty of options for employment in a variety of industries, as opposed to the rather limited economic opportunities of the East Coast urban centers. Many had agricultural or viticultural backgrounds or quickly picked up the trade. By 1859, there were enough Italians in Northern California to support the founding of an Italian-language newspaper, *La Voce del Popolo*.

In Napa, most Italian immigrants were from the north; many intermarried, creating a huge extended family across the county. The Cavagnaro, Carbone and Semorile families were some of the first to build a new life in the Napa Valley, and over time, hundreds more made their homes here. Some lived in Napa Junction or on farms, ranches and vineyards throughout the countryside, but most resided in Napa city. To serve immigrants in Little Italy, as the neighborhood east of downtown became known, early settlers established hotels and saloons along East Third Street. There, recent arrivals could find a bed and a meal while looking for work and saving up enough to get married and acquire a home of their own. Of these establishments, the oldest building still extant is the

The Brooklyn Hotel and Columbo Hotel during an 1890 flood. The Depot Saloon is just off camera to the right. Photographer Etta A. Thompson. *Courtesy of Napa County Historical Society.*

The Roma Hotel and lodgers in Little Italy in 1906. Photographer H.A. Darms. *Courtesy of Napa County Historical Society.*

Brooklyn Hotel at 812–18 Third Street, built in 1870 and run by several generations of the Cavagnaro family.

Over time, new restaurants opened to cater to the growing interest in Italian American food. Malfatti and ravioli gave way to fine dining and greasy pizza pies. Ruffino's, established in 1950, prided itself on its "delicious food cooked by a discriminating chef, served to perfection." Eight years later, Alfred Carsillo moved to Napa from New Jersey and opened one of the first pizza houses in the city, Alfredo's, which served "pizza at its delightful best."

Like every other immigrant group before them, Italians brought with them a love of cooking and a desire to share their gastronomical traditions. Whether pizza or Pecorino Romano, ravioli or risotto, mortadella or malfatti, that Napans eat Italian food at all is due to some very dedicated immigrant cooks.

Chapter 17

The Depot

No history of Italian food in Napa would be complete without the Depot Hotel. It was one of the longest-running restaurants in the county, operating for eighty-one years, and most of that time it was guided by the culinary talents of two Italian immigrant women. It is the quintessential example of classic Italian American dining.

In the 1850s, several members of the Ferroggiaro family left their tiny hometown of Cornega for the seemingly inexhaustible possibilities of California. With them came twenty-year-old Giovanni Baptista, also spelled Giani or Giobani but known as G.B. By 1870, he was a naturalized citizen living in Yuba County and operating a farm, but two years later, he was in San Francisco. Sometime in 1871 or 1872, he and Barbara Vergine Tornari were married, possibly through an arrangement by their families. Known by her Americanized name, Virginia, she had come to Napa with her two sisters, Catarina and Maria, from Corbessasi. She was twenty years G.B.'s junior, yet by all accounts the marriage was a happy one. They went on to have six children, three in San Francisco and three in Napa.

G.B. and Virginia lived in Napa in the 1870s but did not stay. In 1881, they returned and purchased a six-thousand-square-foot empty lot just east of the Napa River in the heart of the town's growing Italian community. From 1878 to 1881, the Washington Hotel stood at that site, conveniently located next to the train depot, but it burned down a few months before the Ferroggiaros bought the land. They erected a new business to which they gave a very practical name: the Depot Saloon.

Many Italian immigrants to the valley stayed at the Depot and eagerly devoured Virginia's cooking, but one visitor in particular enjoyed his meal a little too much. Cayetano Juárez was good friends with the family and often visited the Depot. While eating with the Ferroggiaros one evening in 1883, Cayetano died abruptly at the table from a ruptured blood vessel. According to one of his descendants, Cayetano had often said that when he died, he wanted to go out "eating and with his boots on." He did just that.

After G.B. died in 1890, Virginia managed the saloon herself. She continued to serve meals to patrons and grew fresh ingredients from her vegetable garden at home. Things were fairly quiet except for a shooting incident four years into her tenure. A customer at the bar, John Brocco, paid for his bottle of wine with a twenty-dollar gold piece, so Tony, the eldest Ferroggiaro son, was sent out to get change. Along the way, he got distracted talking about politics with someone. Brocco decided he'd been stiffed and that another man in the bar, Antonio Minetti, was the culprit. In a fit, Brocco shot at Minetti but missed. He was quickly apprehended and tossed in the slammer. Soon after, it came out that he had served time back in Switzerland after murdering his friend and years later had shot at another man in a Vallejo saloon.

The Depot Saloon in the late nineteenth or early twentieth century. *Courtesy of John L. Callan.*

The Ferroggiaro family in 1895. *Front row, left to right*: Louis (Louie), Albert (Nino) and Mary. *Back row*: Antonio (Tony), Edith (Ada), Adelina (Lena) and Victoria (*standing*). *Courtesy of Napa County Historical Society.*

The Ferroggiaro family became a fixture of Napa County history. One of Virginia and G.B.'s sons, Louie, opened the Ferro Glove Company on B Street, which stayed in business from 1926 to 2004. Their granddaughter Virginia Gibb married into the Zeller family, German immigrants who owned the magnificent Palace Hotel in downtown Napa. Another descendant, Fred Ferroggiaro, joined the Bank of Italy in its early years. That morphed into the Bank of America, and in 1954, Fred became chairman of the board. Virginia's sister Caterina married Nicola Carbone. After his death, she married his brother Antonio. The latter Carbone opened a wine cellar and "Italian Garden" on his Coombsville property.

Virginia turned the saloon keys over to a series of proprietors in the early 1900s and focused her energy on her children and grandchildren. In 1925, forty-four years after initially purchasing it, Virginia Ferroggiaro finally sold the Depot Saloon; she was seventy-two and ready to be done with it.

The lucky buyers, Joseph and Theresa Tamburelli, renamed it the Depot Hotel (despite no longer offering rooms to let) and expanded it to a restaurant and small grocery. Both Tamburellis left northern Italy for the United States in about 1906, Joe landing in Connecticut before going west and Theresa in San Francisco. Not long after her arrival, a devastating earthquake rocked the Bay Area. The 7.9 magnitude quake shook the earth for nearly sixty seconds and was felt from southern Oregon to Los Angeles and as far east as central Nevada. Driven from the chaos of ruins and rebuilding, Theresa and her sister Rose Curti sought refuge at Dave Cavagnaro's Brooklyn Hotel. Not long after that, Rose married Fortunato Martini, the owner of the nearby Union Hotel, while Theresa picked up work as a cook, possibly also at the Union. About 1911, Theresa married Joe, and they moved out of the county. He worked a variety of jobs until they returned to Napa and settled in at the Depot.

At this point, Prohibition was in full effect, but that did not stop the Tamburellis or many other Italian immigrants from bootlegging, selling and drinking wine. It was a deeply embedded element of Italian life. Wine was likely introduced to Italy by the Mycenaean Greeks sometime between 1600 and 1100 BCE. The Romans were infamous for their wine consumption, vineyards, bars and thermopolia (the Roman version of fast-food restaurants that also sold wine). Wine was an important component of Catholicism, the traditional religion of most Italian immigrants. So it should be no surprise that many Italian immigrants ignored Prohibition. A

Behind the bar is John Delucca, a professional musician who ran the Depot Saloon in the early 1900s. *Courtesy of Napa County Historical Society.*

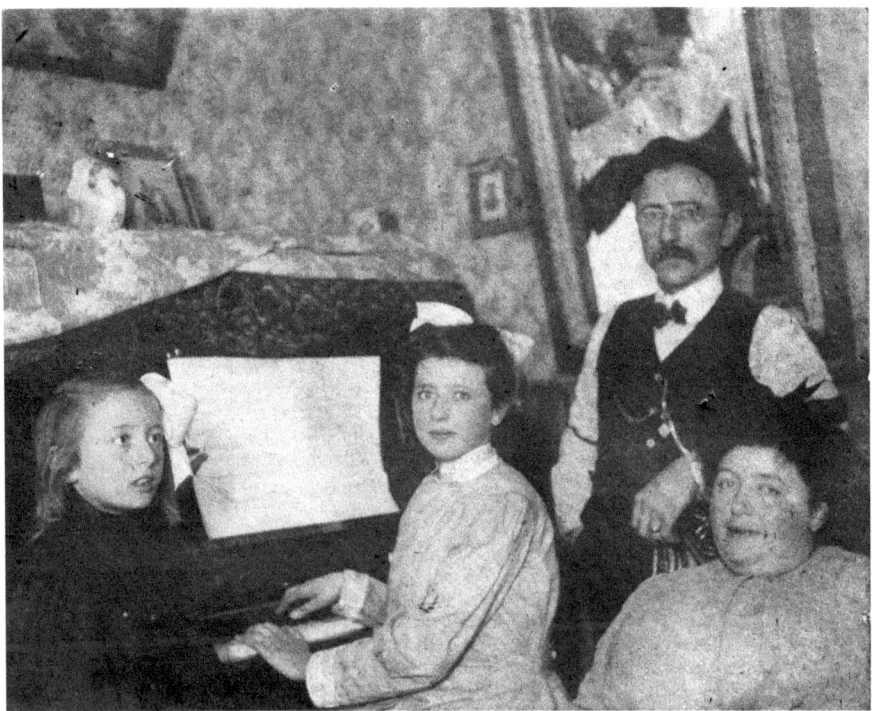

The Delucca family at their piano at the Depot Saloon in the early 1900s. *Left to right*: Irene, Hazel, John and Luisa. *Courtesy of Napa County Historical Society*.

1930 raid by federal agents of several Italian-run hotels in East Napa led to the arrest of four men, Joe Tamburelli included. Thankfully, his charges were dropped after officers could not prove they had purchased liquor at the Depot. He was fined ten dollars for possession of liquor, but without the sale charge, he was safe from jail time.

Besides serving alcohol, the Tamburellis served food at the hotel restaurant just as the Ferroggiaros did. The restaurant had a buffet table as well as tables where diners could be seated and served by a waitress. The exterior left plenty to be desired, but the interior was jam packed with decorations. Inside the sixty-five-seat restaurant was a hodgepodge of mounted heads of deer, several wearing sunglasses, and wallpaper with a hunting motif. Trophies and old photos of the Tamburellis lined the walls. The Depot was a family affair not just for the proprietors but the customers as well, with many returning month after month, year after year.

Theresa was a skilled cook. They regularly advertised her "genuine Italian dinners served every Sunday" and the ravioli and spaghetti she

Dave's Place at the Brooklyn Hotel in 1966. Photographer Charles Loring. *Courtesy of Napa County Historical Society.*

sold as take-out. But she was most famous for her malfatti. If asked, many Napans would claim that malfatti were invented at the Depot. The story has reached legendary status, and the details vary depending on who is telling it. One person might say that in the late 1920s, a baseball team unexpectedly dropped by the restaurant for some of Theresa's ravioli. Another might insist it was a football team and that Theresa had simply forgotten about their reservation. Because it was late in the day, she had run out of a main ingredient for the recipe, either flour or meat. Scrounging to feed the hungry men, she rolled out the filling into small cylinders, boiled them and served them up with a tomato-based sauce. She dubbed her creations *malfatti*, translating to "badly made." The dish was a hit, and soon people were coming from all over just for a taste. Supposedly, the owner of a high-end restaurant in San Francisco tried to convince Theresa to come cook for him, but she refused.

No matter how the story is told, there is one truth: Theresa Tamburelli did not invent malfatti. Malfatti is a type of gnocchi that has been around for a very long time. Even Virginia Ferroggiaro was known for her malfatti. Her great-grandson Robert Zeller wistfully remembered how she made him ravioli and malfatti when he visited her house as a boy.

Theresa certainly put her own spin on the recipe and helped popularize it locally, but the basic dish predates the arrival of a starving sports team by a very long time.

It did not take long for malfatti to make it onto menus of other Napa County Italian restaurants. Edvidge Giometti sold malfatti along with ravioli, taglierini, enchiladas and "green paste" at her restaurant on Main Street, St. Helena, while the Napa Valley Inn offered plates of malfatti, ravioli or fried chicken. Plenty of Napa Valley cooks emulated her recipes, but Theresa kept her crown as the "malfatti queen."

Joe's brother Battista came to work at the restaurant in 1930 after working for many years for the Pacific Portland Cement Company. Daughter Angelina Momsen worked alongside her mother after graduating from Napa High School in 1932 and remained involved in the business until 1998. Son Nicholas helped run the restaurant after his father died in 1937 until about 1974, three years after his mother's death. After that, he and Angelina leased it to her son Howard and Clemente Cittoni.

Clemente, another Italian immigrant who had settled in East Napa, had started as a dishwasher at the Depot in 1961 before moving up to cook. Theresa taught him her personal recipe for malfatti and other dishes, and he made few changes when he took over. In 1979, he offered a five-course dinner for six to ten dollars: soup with "an ample relish tray" and an "infinite supply of Pacini Italian-French bread" came first, then a salad followed by fresh pasta with marinara sauce. The main entrée was a choice between chicken liver, sweetbread, prawns, lamb chops, veal Florentine, saltimbocca, steak or fried chicken. Lastly came dessert of a scoop of ice cream or sherbet. The biggest sellers were ravioli, malfatti and spaghetti; Clemente made about twenty-four thousand pieces of ravioli and malfatti by hand each week. By the 1990s, the Tamburellis had relinquished ownership to Clemente and his new partner, Ronald Martini. The restaurant was voted best Italian food in the city in 1997.

In the early 2000s, the owners closed the restaurant briefly and then sold the business and property to San Francisco restaurateur Russell Kassman. He added an entertainment space dubbed the Rainbow Room to attract new clientele and grew the restaurant and bar menus to offer a wide range of dishes beyond the classic Italian. He also added "the best Jewish deli items west of Manhattan," featuring Kassman's mother's matzo ball soup.

Kassman's gambit was unsuccessful. In 2006, the Depot closed for good. A few eateries have tried to make a go of it in the years since, but none has survived. Once the city tore down the old train depot and a used car lot sprang up around the building, the location became less than ideal for a swinging Italian restaurant. Locals desperate for good old-fashioned Italian food are still in luck. Clemente relocated to the industrial kitchen in the back of Val's Liquors on Third Street, Napa. To this day, he still serves take-out versions of Theresa Tamburelli's malfatti and other tasty Italian treats.

Chapter 18
Napa Raviola and Noodle Parlor

On the ground floor of the Napa Hotel building on the side abutting the Napa Valley Opera House was 1014 Main Street. The address had been home to several restaurants, none of which lasted more than a couple years. The Napa Delicatessen was the first eatery at the site and was run by Mr. and Mrs. H.A. Coles in 1925. They sold not only deli meats from both sides of the Atlantic but also vegetable and potato dishes, pie, salads, ravioli and "the best coffee in town." Diners could order off a lunch menu or pick out a pre-cooked meal. The deli vacated the site the next year and was replaced by Fred and Mildred Blackman's soda shop, Fred's Chili Bowl. That, too, lasted only a short time, and in March 1927, the Daglias opened the Napa Raviola Parlor and Noodle Parlor, also known as the Daglia Ravioli Factory.

Luigi "Louis" Daglia emigrated from Italy in 1896 and within eight years married Erminia Durato, who, like him, was from Lombardy. Louis changed jobs frequently, but by 1907, they had settled in Napa Junction, where he managed the Napa Junction City Hotel and then the Liberal Hotel. In the early 1910s, he briefly took over as proprietor from John Delucca at Virginia Ferroggiaro's Depot Saloon. Then from about 1920 to 1929, he and Louis Zaro, an Italian American born in San Francisco, ran the Progress Grocery on Main and Pearl Streets. The store sold the usual grocery store fare but also catered to the local Italian population with imported groceries from the homeland. In 1929, Daglia sold Zaro his shares and went into the restaurant business.

When this photo was taken by H.A. Darms in 1906, the Daglias' site at the far left was the T Pot Saloon, Charles Baracco proprietor. *Courtesy of Napa County Historical Society.*

The Napa Raviola Parlor offered a robust menu that included Italian dinners, macaroni, roast chicken, roast beef, salads, enchiladas, beans, chili con carne and tamales. Erminia's homemade pasta was the biggest enticement on hand. They sold takeaway orders of six dozen ravioli for only a dollar.

A fire in 1929 nearly cost the Daglias their livelihood. An overheated chimney flue over a stove set fire to the wood beams in the wall before spreading through the kitchen. Fortunately, the damage was minor. Besides the ravioli parlor, only the neighboring barbershop and the cigar store run by Henry "Tupie" Banchero and William "Bill" Litz were affected; the hotel was spared the worst of it.

The Daglias had an on-again-off-again partnership with John and Ruth Maldonado. While working together in 1930, the two couples even lived together in the Daglias' home at 1434 Third Street. John was a cook and Ruth a waitress. The Maldonados ran the ravioli parlor for three months in 1930, and then the Daglias took sole control. Ruth campaigned for Queen of the Elks Italian Pageant in 1928 but lost out to Eleanor Simpkins. Sometime after 1930, Ruth left the ravioli parlor and possibly even her husband. John moved out of the Daglias' home but continued to cook at the restaurant. His rented room was raided by Prohibition agents in July 1932. Two months later, they raided the restaurant and arrested the Daglias' new co-owner, John Capitani. Nothing else is known of the Maldonados. Neither owned any property, nor were they counted on the census records. They disappeared from local newspapers after 1932.

Capitani suffered a series of difficult events that may have led to him finally selling out in 1934. His wife, Amanda, divorced him on grounds of cruelty in 1930. After the Prohibition raid, he was fined fifty dollars.

Five months later, his dog went missing and a tire was stolen off his car. In August 1933, he was arrested for disturbing the peace, and then someone passed a fraudulent check at his restaurant. Meanwhile, he had defaulted on his payments to Napa Building and Loan. By the fall of 1933, Capitani and the Daglias were out of 1014 Main, and the following year, Jew Cheong opened the A-1 Cafe.

Louis and Erminia went on to open the Napa Motel on Soscol Avenue, which they ran for several years. One daughter, Elma, married a Cavagnaro. Both sons played baseball, Pete in the Major Leagues and Andy on local teams. Their ravioli parlor was short-lived, but Napans' love affair with Italian food was only just beginning.

During the mid-twentieth century, Italian food went from "exotic" to "common" much in the same way as Chinese food did during the same period. Pizza became a national favorite as regional variations developed. As more ingredients from different regions in Italy were imported beginning in the 1970s, Italian food began to appear in fine dining establishments. Versatile and appetizing, Italian food is now a staple of the American diet.

Malfatti
Recipe printed in *Il cuoco senza pretese ossia la cucina facile ed economica*, 1826

Spinacci libbra 1
Butiro once 1 e 1/2
Latte 1/2 boccale
Uova N. 2
Formaggio once 1
Sale

Caterina's Parmesan Polenta
Recipe provided by Nichelini Family Winery, 2019

1 cup polenta
6 cups liquid (chicken broth or water)
⅔ cup grated parmesan cheese
Salt to taste

Bring 3 cups of the liquid to a boil. Gradually pour in the polenta, whisking continuously. The liquid will absorb very quickly. Add another cup of liquid, then reduce heat to low. Continue cooking, adding 1 or 2 cups of liquid as it is absorbed. Add the grated parmesan cheese and whisk thoroughly. When desired firmness has been reached, remove and serve. Polenta can be served runny or very firm. When cold can be sliced and fried. Makes 6 servings.

PART VII

EARLY TWENTIETH-CENTURY CLASSICS

Restaurants underwent a major overhaul in the early twentieth century. The 1920 census revealed that for the first time in American history, more people lived in urban areas than rural. Fresh off the boat, European immigrants congregated in cities. African Americans fled racial and economic strife in the South for the North, Midwest and West; 1.6 million left between 1916 and 1940, with another 5 million striking out during and after World War II. All this movement brought change and conflict. Racism, fascism and nativism ramped up in response to unchecked capitalism and demands for social reform. Economic collapse and two massive wars forever changed the world, and civil rights movements strived to improve it.

As people clustered in cities, lunch counters, cafeterias and delicatessens cropped up to feed the mass of hungry workers who needed a quick, cheap lunch. Restaurants changed little in their physical layout, but the dishes served were updated to contemporary palates and expanded to include newly introduced foods from other cultures. Office workers and businesspeople in downtown Napa flocked to the Berlin Cafe and Marino's Grill for their cheap merchant's lunches and mouthwatering dinners, while Japanese Americans C.M. Kitoku (or Kitoka) and J. Nankagawa served oysters and tamales at the California Restaurant.

For many Napans, the sociocultural issues raging around the world seemed distant, but in truth, they were right in front of them. The demographics were changing, albeit slowly, and the county was about to hit a major growth spurt. The two

Interior of Bryant's Candy Shop in the Gordon Building on First Street, Napa, 1928. *Courtesy of Diane R. Adams.*

restaurants featured here operated just before and right at the start of this new era. They act as bridges between tradition and avant-garde, the familiar and the unknown, the "always was" and the "coming soon."

Chapter 19
Mrs. Tobin's Restaurants

Sometime in the 1860s, Michael and Mary Tobin arrived in Napa. Mary was born in New York to Irish parents, while Michael had just sailed across the Atlantic from Ireland. Michael was a gardener before eventually opening a nursery on Vallejo Street. Mary contented herself with keeping house for the first years of marriage, but she had an adventurous spirit. In 1878, she leased a store on Main Street near the First Street Bridge, where she set up an ice cream parlor. Besides homemade ice cream, she also sold fruit and confectionery (an old-fashioned word for candies and pastries). The following year, she changed venues as well as foods when she opened a "Coffee Stand and Refreshment Saloon." She kept this eatery until at least 1880.

In 1883, she purchased Joseph A. Horrel's restaurant on Main Street (where the parking lot is between the Winship Building and Downtown Joe's today). The interior was nicely decorated with ferns, geraniums and begonias—hardly surprising given her husband's occupation. Like many restaurants of the day, she served oysters in a variety of styles, as well as clam chowder, beef and chicken tamales and homemade ice cream. She was known for her enticing window displays of the succulent roast meats she served for dinner. Raved a reporter for the *Napa Journal*, "It would make even a dyspeptic's mouth water to look at the nice fat turkeys, ducks, geese, chickens, porkers, etc., that she has on exhibition."

She briefly closed in the spring of 1893 to visit family back east and then reopened in the relatively new Winship Building, just a few doors up from her old location. This site was larger, with a spacious main dining room, three private family rooms and intimate boxes for a solo diner or a couple. The kitchen was in a separate building added to the back of the restaurant and was fitted up with "a speaking tube and electric bells" so the front of house could pass orders to the kitchen staff.

Tom McGill was the head steward at both locations. His parents were Irish immigrants who settled in Baltimore. In the 1870s, he made his way to Napa, where he soon got a job at the Revere House and there met Mary. Together, they managed the hotel for a few years, and then he joined her restaurant. He was so dedicated that he did not take a single vacation for eleven years.

By March 1898, Mary and Michael were ready for a change of scenery. She sold her restaurant to E. Himmel, who had been running the Mississippi Kitchen in Sacramento, and decided to open a business in

Close-up of Mrs. Tobin's Restaurant from an 1889 illustration of Napa by E.S. Moore. *Courtesy of Napa County Historical Society.*

Early Twentieth-Century Classics

Right: The Revere House, to the left of the Masonic Temple, in 1906. Photographer H.A. Darms. *Courtesy of Napa County Historical Society.*

Below: The Popular Dining Room took over Mrs. Tobin's former site at 13–15 South Main Street in 1906. One of the men is probably the proprietor, Louis Hirsch, a twenty-seven-year-old Austrian Jew. Photographer H.A. Darms. *Courtesy of Napa County Historical Society.*

Alaska. This may seem like an odd choice, but gold had been discovered two years prior in the Yukon Territory, and the region was flooded with prospectors and businesspeople eager to make it rich. It would have been a lucky move had they left as planned, for gold was discovered in Nome in the fall of that year. Tragically, Michael died suddenly a month after Mary closed the restaurant.

After dealing with her late husband's estate, Mary finally moved to Nome, but her dreams of running a restaurant there withered on the vine. Nome was absolutely teeming with people and businesses; carving out a niche was nearly impossible. Mary mined her claims in the summer and worked as a housekeeper in winter. For women trying to make a go of it in Alaska, the work was difficult and the wages lower than elsewhere in the United States. When asked about her time there, Mary offered a quote from another woman who had moved to Alaska and lived to tell her tale to the *Seattle Post-Intelligencer*: "Alaska is not a place for women who expect to grow rich quickly and to accomplish that in competition with men."

After a life of excitement and enterprise, she passed away in 1911 at sixty-seven. Like many woman restaurateurs, Mary was a dauntless figure. She knew what she wanted out of life and went for it. She did not defy the assumption of the era of what a "proper" lady should be so much as redefine it. She was neither the first woman restaurant owner in Napa County nor the last, but she did leave an impression.

Chapter 20
Classic Grill

Decades of economic and political turmoil left Greece struggling in the early 1900s. Perhaps that is why the Smerneadis brothers—Dionisios and older brothers Antone, Nick and Pete—left their home in Filiatra. Dionisios Americanized his name to Daniel Smernes and joined his brother Tony in the United States in 1906 when he was about sixteen; the others arrived after. No one is quite sure what they did to occupy their time, but they likely worked in Sacramento restaurants. For at least ten years, Dan owned and managed a restaurant in Chicago.

In early 1922, Dan and Pete moved to Napa and opened a restaurant on Main Street near First called Classic Grill. About the same time, they also opened Classic Grills in Santa Rosa and Vallejo. Tony operated the Vallejo branch, but he also got into wrestling promotion in 1932. About a month after opening the Classic Grill in Napa, Dan returned to Sacramento to marry Olga Lambropulos (or Lambros), who had emigrated from Filiatra in 1915.

The Classic Grill served meals similar to other restaurants of the period. A merchant's lunch of soup, salad, entrée, dessert and coffee, milk or tea could be had for forty-five cents, or a diner could splurge on Sunday dinner for one dollar. The latter's bill of fare changed regularly. One weekend there was a relish dish of radishes and ripe olives, chicken broth with rice, a "combination salad," filet of sole with tartar sauce, roast chicken with dressing, chicken fricassee with asparagus, roast beef sirloin with "Spanish sauce," potatoes au gratin, peas and ice cream with

Left: Olga and Dan Smernes in the late 1920s or early 1930s. *Courtesy of Jeanette Mulgrew.*

Below: Plates and napkins from the Classic Grill. Olga and Dan acquired the small handkerchiefs while on their honeymoon. *Courtesy of Jeanette Mulgrew and the author.*

wafers. A month later, the options included "chicken malacatone" soup, fried salmon with lemon butter sauce, chicken fricassee with sweet corn, homemade chicken stew, fried chicken à la cream, roast stuffed chicken, mashed potatoes, carrots in cream and vanilla ice cream. In the late 1920s and early 1930s, Dan chose a slogan that would surely land him in hot water today: "If your wife can't cook, don't divorce her—Keep her for a pet and eat WITH US."

The restaurant was so successful that in 1927, Dan pulled together $40,000 (almost $600,000 today) to purchase the Winship Building at Main and First Streets. Thereafter, the Winship was known as the Smernes Building; the name only reverted when it was put on the city's Historical Resources Inventory in the 1970s. Dan rightly predicted that property values would increase and owning "one of the finest and most desirable [blocks] in the business district" would pay dividends in the future.

Pete decided to stake his own claim on success and get married. He sailed home with Nick Captain, a Greek friend and cook in Vallejo. Although both were in their late forties, they wed women twenty years their junior. A year later, in 1930, Pete split from Dan. He took over the restaurant in the Napa Hotel building and opened Pete's Grill. In it he "installed the finest equipment and secured the best assistants to conduct his grill along high class lines." Everything in it was "entirely new and modern in every way." His business partner was Tony Stikos, a Greek cook from Sacramento. Stikos whipped up fare not all that different from the Classic Grill: soup, salad, chicken dinner and dessert. Capitalizing on his proximity to hotel guests and Opera House performers, Pete secured an appearance from Bull Montana, also known as Lewis or Luigi Montagna, an Italian immigrant wrestler and silent movie actor.

In the 1930s, the Classic Grill served a chicken dinner, merchant's lunch, eggs with ham or bacon, tomato star noodle soup, sugar beet salad, entrées of roast spring chicken served family style, baked chicken, small club steak, chicken liver omelette and desserts like strawberry shortcake, pudding or fruit jello. Waffles and hot cakes made their way onto the menu by 1931, as did broiled lobster with chili sauce and cracked crab with mayonnaise.

Dan relocated the Classic Grill once, in 1933, but only two doors down. As he went from a rental into the building he now owned, the move was very convenient. With the better location, he decided to start fresh and switch the name to Golden Glow Inn. Patronage may have dropped off as a result, or perhaps Dan simply grew nostalgic. Either way, the Classic Grill name was restored a few months later.

Above: In white and seated at the bar is Pete Smernes, taken at the opening of Tupie's Tavern in 1938. Run by Bill Litz (wearing a hat) and Tupie Banchero (behind the bar wearing a black tie), the tavern replaced Pete's Grill. *Courtesy of Napa County Historical Society*.

Opposite, top: The Classic Grill in the Smernes Building in the late 1930s. *Courtesy of Jeanette Mulgrew*.

Opposite, bottom: Dan Smernes, *far left*, behind the bar in the Classic Grill in the late 1930s. For couples or solo diners wanting privacy, there were booths between tables that could be closed off with curtains. *Courtesy of Jeanette Mulgrew*.

Early Twentieth-Century Classics

Tragedy struck the Smernes family over and over again. In 1923, Olga and Dan's first child, Amphetrete, died at just forty days old; Olga also suffered a miscarriage. A few months later, Jason Korekas, one of their cooks at the Napa and Santa Rosa restaurants, drowned in the ocean in Santa Cruz not far from where Olga and Dan honeymooned the summer before. Jason was on his own honeymoon with Edna Hardin barely a week after signing the marriage license in Napa. His body was never recovered. In 1926, Dan's brother Nick suffered a stroke or cerebral hemorrhage and died after spending several days unconscious. The following year, another brother, Frank, was brutally shot to death over a dispute during a Greek card game. Frank worked in the Classic Grill before moving to Vallejo to open the Athens Pool Hall. The killer, James Lazarus, was convicted of first-degree murder and sentenced to life in prison at San Quentin.

In 1934, Dan backed away from the Napa restaurant to help run his brother's Vallejo restaurant. Brothers Larry and Sam Agnello took over and brought in chef Martin Sundy. The Agnellos and Sunday were out by the fall of 1935 as Dan reasserted his ownership. The following spring, Dan purchased the Napa Hotel and undertook extensive renovations. Pete ran his restaurant under his brother's watchful eye for a few more years before he and his wife, Bessie (or Billie), moved to Sacramento and then back to Greece.

Dan kept the Classic Grill a little while longer but in 1939 gave it over to Pete Sanders. By 1941, the restaurant was gone, and the Smernes Building turned over to medical and professional offices and retail. Dan died in 1947 after rejecting his doctor's advice to eat healthier. Olga still spoke mostly only Greek and struggled after her husband's death. She had relied on him to manage the family finances and business affairs, but now she had to learn how to do everything on top of taking care of her five children. But Olga carried on, as women often do. After earning citizenship, seeing several of her children happily married and becoming a grandmother, Olga passed in 1968.

Ice Cream with Variations
Recipe printed in the *Napa Journal*, 1900

The plain cream is liked by most people better than the cooked custard. To make it use three pints of cream to one pint of milk, and one three-quarters cups of sugar. Scald the milk, melt the sugar in it, and when it is cool add the mixture to the cream. If vanilla is the flavor required, add a tablespoonful of the extract, or of the pounded vanilla bean, sugar; if lemon, a tablespoonful of the extract. For pistachio ice cream blanch and pound to a paste three-quarters of a cup of pistachio nuts and one-quarter of a cup of almonds. Any fruit may be used, such as strawberries, peaches, raspberries, pineapples, cherries, apricots and bananas, by mashing them thoroughly and adding them after the cream is partly frozen; for coffee three-quarters quart of cream, omitting the milk in the foregoing rule.

Chocolate flavor may be obtained by melting two squares of chocolate and stirring it smooth in a little of the milk and adding to the milk cream and sugar.

Sautéed Chicken
Recipe by Judith Wilson, reprinted in the *Napa Journal*, 1934

Select and saute the breasts in melted butter with twelve mushroom caps until browned, then add one cup hot chicken broth, two ounces sherry and two cups cream. Season with salt, pepper and paprika and cook gently about ten minutes. Season three cups cooked egg noodles with salt, pepper and Parmesan cheese and arrange in a casserole. Place the chicken breasts on top of the noodles and the mushrooms on the chicken. Cook down the sauce in which the chicken was cooked, strain and thicken with two egg yolks. Pour over the chicken and place under a flame to brown.

PART VIII

MID-CENTURY MODERN

IN MANY WAYS, THE HISTORY OF THE UNITED STATES IS THE history of beef. In the West, as territory was commandeered from sovereign Indigenous nations, first by the Spanish and Mexican and later by Americans, it was reshaped into grazing land for cattle. Alta California's economy was based almost exclusively on the variety of materials and foodstuffs produced from butchered cows. As American cowboys moved across the plains, the beef cattle they raised lined the pockets of wealthy ranchers and filled the bellies of the soldiers who brutally enforced American dominance. Beef production profitability soared again with the spread of the railroads and the concentration of industrialized slaughterhouses in urban centers. By the late nineteenth century, nearly every American regardless of economic status regularly ate beef. By the early 1900s, Americans ate 40 to 50 pounds of beef per person every year. Starting in 1932, the per capita consumption rates began to rise, reaching a shocking 91.5 pounds in 1976.

Unsurprisingly, nearly all of Napa's mid-century restaurants had beef on the menu. Many served it in a dish that is as American as chili and chop suey: the hamburger. The name is derived from the city of Hamburg, Germany, although the dish's Germanic connections are arguable. There are at least five possible origin stories, most involving European immigrants experimenting with American foodstuff. However the hamburger came to be, its popularity cannot be denied. With the influx of automobiles came the drive-in and drive-through. Fast-food chains and burger stands appeared, and the

Actress Carole Lombard having breakfast at the Plaza Hotel restaurant with Napa Chamber of Commerce representative Charles Grady. She was in town shooting scenes for the 1940 film *They Knew What They Wanted*. *Courtesy of Napa County Historical Society.*

Undated photograph of workers repaving the parking lot of the Wright Spot, a drive-in on Soscol Avenue. *Courtesy of Napa County Historical Society.*

humble hamburger became synonymous with quick and cheap dining. More advanced and efficient equipment made it easier to produce burgers and the now-standard accompaniments of French fries and milkshakes.

Napa's sit-down restaurants and take-out joints had a harmonious relationship during the mid-twentieth century. Teenagers hung out at drive-ins like Lily's, Kenny's, Knotty Pine and Chic's Burgers, while workers and neighbors took advantage of the filling dishes at Nu Way Drug Fountain and the Highway 29 Cafe. There were so few restaurants in the county prior to the 1970s that both could coexist without pilfering customers from each other. The wine revolution of the 1970s brought with it thousands of new tourists and residents and a great demand for more restaurants and different or more upscale menus. Napa's restaurateurs asked themselves if simple, classic, American-style eateries could live alongside or even outlast the demand for haute cuisine. For older restaurants rooted in the classic and simple American-style menu, the answer was all too frequently "no."

Chapter 21
Jonesy's Famous Steak House

Wisconsinite Hugh Jones moved to Napa County in 1923 with big dreams. In 1927, he married Ethel Cavagnaro and picked up work here and there as a driver and tanner at Sawyer Tanning Company, a chauffeur for Superior Court judge Henry C. Gesford and assorted jobs at Mare Island Naval Station.

With the United States' entry into World War II in 1941, the U.S. Army Corps of Engineers set up an auxiliary air defense field to train pilots for a possible invasion by the Japanese. After the war ended in 1945, the military shed its surplus wartime properties, and suddenly the county government found itself in possession of an airfield. A year later, the county held a grand opening for the brand-new municipal airport. Inside, Bill Longhurst set up a small concession stand with eleven stools for guests and a hot plate and a coffee maker as the makeshift kitchen, but he did not stick around. Hugh and Ethel moved in and established Jonesy's Steak and Chicken House, later known as Jonesy's Famous Steak House.

Their restaurant was hit from the beginning. The first month, they worked almost nonstop and pulled in $325 (about $4,000 today). They added a four-top table the following year to accommodate more patrons and expanded again when a new terminal building was added. But on May 28, 1952, they suffered a major setback. About 5:30 a.m., a fire believed to be caused by burglars broke out in the administration building. Flames leveled the Southwest Airways offices and control tower, the Bridgeford Flying Service offices and Jonesy's. Everything in the kitchen and dining room was ruined, as were the jukebox and pinball machine.

The county immediately set to repairs. Oakland architect Russell deLappe designed the new building to be constructed out of strestcrete, fireproof concrete blocks developed and trademarked by Basalt Rock Company, a cement producer and shipyard just up the road from the airport. At Jonesy's reopening in the spring of 1953, diners sat in front of the new windows facing the landing strip and indulged in sirloin club, steak fillet, New York steak, hamburgers, sandwiches, rolls, dessert of ice cream or sherbet and Jonesy's special potatoes. Composed of grilled and shredded potatoes with a hunk of melted American cheese and grilled onions, the special potatoes were a must-have. Supposedly the recipe originated from the grandmother of Hugh's good friend Don Townsend. She prepared her breakfast potatoes for friends and family every Sunday, and Hugh couldn't get enough of them. Salads came with Jonesy's famous blue cheese dressing, which was so popular it was bottled and sold in local grocery stores.

Hugh had a rather unusual grilling technique for his steaks: he sandwiched the meat between the grill and heavy, seasoned rocks plucked from the Sacramento River. *Napa Register* columnist Jim Ford claimed Hugh got the idea from Jane Greenwood Bishop, the wife of the airport's first manager. In one memorable instance, an official with the Mexican consular office demanded his steak cooked well-done. Hugh, who always cooked steaks rare, was not having it. Instead of the well-done steak, Hugh put one of the river rocks on a plate and sent it out of the kitchen. The taunt came back to haunt him a few months later when Hugh was detained while trying to fly into Mexico without the proper paperwork. The official sent to sort everything out was none other than the man Hugh had clashed with. Luckily, he found the whole thing hilarious and helped Hugh anyway.

The entire Jones family threw themselves into the restaurant. Ethel, having attended Napa Business College, had the managerial know-how. She managed the staff, organized reservations, ordered supplies and handled other day-to-day work. Hugh's "knowledge of the culinary arts [was] second to none," so he was usually stationed at the grill in his chef whites and a two-foot-tall toque blanche. Their son Hugh Jr. also worked in the kitchen as a cook, and daughter Yvonne worked as a hostess.

Hugh was a gregarious and gracious man adored by almost everyone. He frequently left the grill to greet guests in the dining room with the nicknames he bestowed on people he liked. At the end of each dinner shift, he made sure even the oft-ignored dishwashers got a full meal. Staff at Jonesy's were,

Mid-Century Modern

Left: A framed drawing of Hugh Jones Sr. with a plate of special potatoes served on the original dishware. *Courtesy of Kimberly Wilkinson and the author.*

Below: The Joneses purchasing a 1956 Chrysler from Gasser Motors. *From left to right*: Yvonne Jones, Hugh Jones Jr., Joan Jones, Peter A. Gasser, Hugh Jones Sr., Ethel Jones and Ralph Armstrong. *Courtesy of Napa County Historical Society.*

according to Yvonne, "a fiercely loyal crew.... They were there for years and years and years. It was just like one big family."

Jonesy's was the kind of place "people always come back again and again.... The management has endeavored to make constant improvement so that your each successive visit is even more of a treat than the previous one." The menu was simple but deliciously filling. When advertisements proclaimed the restaurant "a West Coast favorite for excellent cuisine," they were not exaggerating. By the mid-1960s, 225,000 people ate at Jonesy's every year. Most were from the area, but about 20 percent flew in from elsewhere. Small aircraft pilots made a point of popping by whenever possible. A pilot named Harry Doose claimed to have eaten 1,300 meals there between 1954 and 1966.

Over the years, hundreds of famous people passed through Jonesy's doors. Bay Area real estate developers Al Stern and Dick Price, golfer Arnold Palmer, TV anchor Dave McElhatton, prolific film and television actor Robert Taylor, Fess Parker (star of television shows *Daniel Boone* and *Davy Crockett*), Joe E. Brown of *Some Like It Hot*, Danny Kaye, Jimmy Stewart, Shirley Temple, Bette Midler, Robert Redford, Goldie Hawn, Kurt Russell and former governor Jerry Brown all visited. Paul Newman supposedly sent a helicopter to collect an order of twenty-five hamburgers. When John Wayne stopped by, he apparently required his friends to each order a steak sandwich, which they devoured while watching football on a television propped up on one of the tables.

A matchbook from Jonesy's. *Courtesy of Todd L. Shulman.*

Hugh and Ethel endured many ups and downs. Fifteen years after the fire, in 1967, Ethel died of cancer. A year later, Hugh remarried, this time to Napan Rowena Jensen. Not long after that, Hugh was featured in a series on the Sacramento TV station KCRA titled *The Man Who Went to Dinner*. He hit another roadblock during the meat shortage of 1973. Beef prices had been rising due to increased production and feed costs, triggering a weeklong consumer boycott in April. President Richard Nixon fixed meat prices in an attempt to ease the problem, but the shortage continued through the fall. For Hugh, the choice was to take his vacation a few weeks early or stay open and either raise dinner prices or cut his profit margin. He chose the vacation.

Things were going well after the shortage when his 250- to 300-seat restaurant was pulling in about $1 million in annual gross. Then in 1976, Hugh fell ill. He passed managerial duties over to meat cutter and cook Everett "Pinky" Dering. After several months of hospitalization, Hugh died in January 1977. The restaurant closed for a day to honor his memory.

William "Bill" and Dorothy "Dotty" Tuthill, Pinky and Pearl Dering and Lee and Florence "Flo" Carbone took over Jonesy's a month later. Pinky and Bill had been with the restaurant for most of its run and knew the business inside and out. The Tuthills gradually bought out the others to become the sole owners. They renovated and expanded the restaurant, sinking in nearly $400,000 in improvements. The Napa County Airport was also bringing in waves of cash. By the late 1980s, there were fifty hangars housing nearly $17 million worth of aircraft. Airport enterprises brought in $450,000 in annual revenue plus another $250,000 in taxes.

Unfortunately, the bubble was about to burst. Foot and flight traffic were in decline by the mid-1990s. With Bill managing operations and Pinky running the kitchen, the restaurant still had a draw. They kept the feel of old-school Jonesy's but grew the menu to include seafood, more salads and a wider range of lunch options. In 1998, Napans voted Jonesy's the best restaurant for business. A decade later, Jonesy's served about two thousand people a week, which sounds like a lot but is only about half as many as in the 1960s.

Bill retired in 2009 and sold the restaurant to Nancy and Terry Otton. Napans, like many people in close-knit communities, can be slow to accept change. When Bill departed, longtime diner Susan Fontana expressed the worry many Jonesy's fans had: "There are some places that don't change, and Jonesy's is one of them." Change came anyway.

Ironically, in 1971, Napa County Airport, which began as an airfield for pilots to practice repelling the Japanese air force, entered into a contract with Japan Airlines and the International Air Service Company (IASCO), which trained pilots from Japan and other countries. The JAL made up 15 percent of the airport revenue and 50 percent of all flights. They even built a condominium complex in north Napa for the 250 or so employees and their families. When the JAL collapsed in 2010 and IASCO in 2012, the drastic drop in revenue hit the airport hard. Amid all this, Nancy and Terry were trying desperately to keep Jonesy's afloat. They revitalized the restaurant and held special dining events. They upped the quality of the ingredients, tweaked the recipe for the special potatoes and added contemporary dishes to the classic menu. The portions got smaller as the wine list grew longer, but it was not enough. The Ottons lasted less than a year before closing Jonesy's for good.

Jonesy's existed from 1946 to 2010. Known by pilots around the globe, it had a devoted following. In the words of Beverly Brown Healey, a pilot at Bridgeford in the 1970s, Jonesy's was "a warm, family-friendly place to share lunch with other pilots.…As often as possible we got a table by the window so that we could watch the airplanes or in the evening watch the sunset. It was my pleasure to have eaten there many times."

Chapter 22
Taylor's Refresher

As you enter St. Helena while driving north on Highway 29, you might notice a sign for Taylor's Refresher. Dangling over the sidewalk in front of Gott's Roadside restaurant, the sign's bright yellow letters are fading in the sun and the painted burger, fries and lemonade are cracking. Erected in 1974, the sign stands sentry over a restaurant consigned to history.

The origins of one of the most beloved restaurants in St. Helena began, rather incongruously, with a gravel company. A gravel plant opened on Skellenger Lane near Rutherford in 1929. Thomas F. McGill (no relation to Tom McGill of Mrs. Tobin's Restaurant) and his son Harold took over the plant in 1932 and renamed it the McGill Rock and Sand Company. They dredged gravel out of Conn Creek and dumped it into their massive machinery, which in turn produced crushed rock. From that, cement, ready-mixed concrete, gravel, sand and other construction materials were made. McGill concrete was even used to build the new St. Helena City Hall in 1955.

In 1947, Thomas traded his home in Vallejo for two acres or so of land on Main Street at the south end of St. Helena. Before the deal was finalized, he convinced the city to allow him to straighten out a dangerous curve at that part of the road, realign and widen the bridge over Sulphur Creek, straighten the creek and fill in the former waterway, all at his own expense.

Thomas died two years later, and while Harold got the gravel business, Thomas's daughter Marion Taylor inherited the St. Helena property. Her late father had plans to develop the site, and Marion and her husband,

Lloyd, known as Popsie, had relocated from Nebraska to help him manage everything. Lloyd had no background in restaurants; in Kearney he was a pharmacist, realtor and insurance salesman. While Lloyd had the business experience, Marion had the culinary knowledge. After graduating from UC Santa Barbara and UC Berkeley, she began work at Taft High School, where she instituted one of California's first school lunch programs. The couple had been looking forward to retirement, but after exploring root beer stands and burger joints in Fresno and Visalia, they were inspired to build one in St. Helena.

Taylor's Refresher opened in late 1949, but the grand opening of "St. Helena's most modern drive-in" took place on June 23, 1950. All afternoon guests were treated to free Lyons root beer. Diners parked and gave orders to a carhop or walked up to the counter in the little red-and-white building filled with "the latest stainless steel devices for production of food and soft drinks, including a popcorn gadget of some intricacy."

The burger stand was an instant success. It probably did not hurt that it offered frequent discounts, freebies and other inducements. For years, locals bought Fourth of July fireworks from a stand on the property. The restaurant was also a major employer for St. Helena teenagers. By 1964, it had hired a whopping sixty-three high school students since opening, and countless more came through in subsequent years.

Taylor's Refresher in the late 1950s or early 1960s. *Courtesy of the Taylor family archives.*

The menu in the early years was simple and familiar: hamburgers and cheeseburgers, hot dogs, French fries, popcorn, milkshakes, root beer and root beer floats. Milkshakes "made with the finest of flavors and blended together in our Taylor Shake Machine" were so thick they had to be served with a spoon. But it was the root beer float with two scoops of ice cream and the hamburgers made from two portions of high-quality beef that pulled in the crowds. In the 1960s, the menu of frozen treats expanded to include orange freezes, chocolate frosties and banana splits. Fresh corn, melons, tomatoes and blackberries picked from the bushes along the creek were available during the summer months, as well as milkshakes made with fresh peaches, bananas and strawberries.

On Marion's insistence, the ingredients were fresh, equipment top of the line and service inviting. Everything was prepared by hand. To make fries, an employee hauled in sacks of potatoes from where they were stored

Taylor's Refresher in the early 1950s. *Courtesy of the Taylor family archives.*

Popsie working in the restaurant kitchen, circa 1950s. *Courtesy of the Taylor family archives.*

in the garage to the kitchen. The potatoes were washed and peeled by hand and then put in the fry cutter. But to get from the kitchen to the garage, employees had to maneuver through the gaggle of territorial geese that lived on the property. To the guests they were a fun addition, but to the staff they were, as Lloyd's daughter Jean Taylor Nicholson put it, an "occupational hazard." One afternoon the geese escaped, and Lloyd and his son-in-law Dean Nicholson were summoned to retrieve them. The men stopped traffic on Main Street and walked the birds down the center of the road back to Taylor's.

After Marion's death in 1954, her daughters and sons-in-law Virginia and Charley and Jean and Dean Nicholson brought their families to St. Helena during the busy summer months to help their father with the

Mid-Century Modern

Aunt Minnie, second wife of Tom McGill, playing near the apple trees behind Taylor's with her grandson Bob Nicholson, 1952. *Courtesy of the Taylor family archives.*

Sara and Salinda Toogood enjoying their burgers in the late 1960s. *Courtesy of the Taylor family archives.*

Popsie was quite the animal lover. He had a German shepherd named Josh that he loved dearly and an Arabian horse named Sonny. *Courtesy of the Taylor family archives.*

restaurant. The sisters often worked behind the counter while Charley and Popsie managed the rest of the business.

Charley had an interesting background. Born in Nebraska, he played college football at the University of Nebraska. He was drafted by the Los Angeles Rams and led the team to victory in the 1951 National Football League Championship. After his retirement in 1957, Charley partnered with Glen Bell, Harland Savare and Phil Crosby (son of Bing Crosby) and opened a fast-food Mexican restaurant chain called El Taco. Later, Bell branched out on his own and established the Taco Bell chain. Meanwhile, Charley and Virginia were increasingly discontent with the hectic pace of Southern California. They decided to move with their four children back to Nebraska but offered to stop in St. Helena for a bit to help Popsie. They loved the valley so much they never left. Soon Charley got a job teaching and coaching at St. Helena High School.

Popsie retired in the 1970s and passed the operation on to Virginia and Charley. To commemorate the change, a new sign was commissioned. It was the first commercial job for Bob Zagar, a cabinetmaker with a passion for woodworking. Zagar went on to make signs for other restaurants, fire departments, businesses and private citizens around the country, not to mention local wineries like Charles Krug, Beringer, Louis M. Martini, Inglenook and Christian Brothers (today the home of the Culinary Institute of America). Under Charley and Virginia's guidance, the bill of fare expanded. The menu was shaped as much by the Taylor family as it was by the staff and community. From Charley came burritos and tacos. A Seventh-day Adventist woman from Angwin provided the veggie burger recipe. Pritchard Hill winemaker Donn Chappellet suggested a bacon nut burger that, as Jean recalled, was "a favorite for not only the Chappellets but for us and many customers….It was good!"

The Taylors were always searching for ways to get the most use out of their property. Lloyd built the city's first—and for many years only—car wash and dubbed himself the "Hamburger and Car Wash King of St. Helena." In 1973, the Taylors tried to partner with the Jacob Oil Company to install a full-service gas station near the restaurant but were denied by city council. A decade later, they got approval for a different expansion, this time for a deli and fruit stand. They also opened the Creekside Inn Bed & Breakfast on the property. A decade after that, their request to install a drive-through window was rejected by city officials. By that point, the restaurant sat 125 people and was one of the most popular drive-ins in the county.

For Taylor's, change came in 1999. Virginia and Jean leased the restaurant to brothers Joel and Duncan Gott. They switched the name to Taylor's Automatic Refresher and updated the restaurant equipment and bill of fare. Besides the classic dishes, the menu featured grilled quail, seared tuna tacos, fried mahi mahi, ahi burgers with ginger wasabi mayonnaise and "Asian-style" coleslaw, chili cheese fries, Philly cheesesteaks, verde chicken sandwiches with poblano chile and curried vegetable soup with coconut milk. And a variety of wines and draft beers.

Taylor's became a haven for the gastronomically inclined. "The menu is an eclectic mix of the traditional and the trendy. This is a place that a foodie will enjoy. Everything is downright scrumptious," wrote the *Napa Register*'s food critic. The Gotts won numerous awards for their work at Taylor's, and the high praise kept coming. Influential wine critic Robert Parker named it one of his most memorable meals of 1999, declaring their burgers and shakes "the finest…money can buy." Soon, three hundred guests were visiting during the week and twice that on weekends. Rolling with their success, the brothers opened a second Taylor's in the San Francisco Ferry Building in 2002 and a third at the newly developed Oxbow Public Market in 2006.

A skirmish over branding erupted in 2010 when the Gotts abruptly changed the name to Gott's Roadside Tray Gourmet. Many locals were

A local family friend standing under the Taylor's Refresher sign in the late 1970s. *Courtesy of the Taylor family archives.*

furious at the switch, as was the Taylor family. Virginia and Jean pushed back hard: "Taylor's Refresher has a long and cherished history in St. Helena that will be irreparably damaged by this. This is like changing the name of the Martini Winery, the French Laundry or any other historic business in our community without consent. It's not right. We own the property and the name, not the Gotts." Eventually, the controversy died down, and the Gotts and Taylor family came to a place of understanding. Over time, the name was pared down to Gott's Roadside. Yet to this day, many locals still think of the St. Helena location as Taylor's.

The sign for Taylor's Refresher still swings as a landmark, but what made Taylor's *Taylor's* had ceased to be long before the Gotts ditched the name. Taylor's was no longer a cheap joint to get a tasty burger and frosty root beer float but a gourmet roadside restaurant with wine and an upscale menu. Gott's Roadside is on the list for many tourists and locals alike, but many still long for the classic drive-in days.

Chapter 23
Palby's

Palby's was the kind of restaurant everyone ate at or wanted to. The price was affordable, portions filling, venue spacious, owners welcoming and animal attractions enticing. And when it closed its doors in 2003, it was, as the *Napa Register* put it, the "end of an era in American Canyon."

The American Canyon region of south Napa County was for thousands of years home to the Southern Patwin. During the 1830s and 1840s, it was the site of several battles from the so-called Indian Wars. General Mariano Vallejo, Colonel Salvador Vallejo, Cayetano Juárez and George Yount fought the Southern Patwin under the Mexican flag.

The railroad appeared in the late 1800s, and then manufacturing. Standard Portland Cement opened about 1906, and for the next thirty-two years, 150 employees cranked out two hundred barrels a day of limestone extracted from the quarry. This material was used in countless Bay Area construction projects, including numerous San Francisco buildings after the 1906 earthquake. The ruins of the company can still be seen from South Napa Junction Road, just up the way from where Palby's once stood. The Leslie Salt Company moved in in the mid-twentieth century and converted much of the western wetlands into processing and collection areas for salt production. The site finally shuttered in the 1990s, and environmental agencies have been hard at work trying to restore the marshes.

Despite the activity, growth was minimal by the time Clemence and John Freskan moved in. John was a Greek immigrant who came to the United

American Canyon in 1997 with Standard Portland Cement at far left. *Courtesy of Napa County Historical Society.*

States at fourteen. He met Clemence during World War I when he was sent to fight in France. In 1924, his job with the Southern Pacific Company brought him to Napa Junction, the name for the part of American Canyon near where the Walmart shopping center is today. They opened a grocery store, dance hall and gas station at the corner of South Napa Junction Road and the highway.

After their son Peter graduated from Napa Union High School in 1939, he married his classmate and the girl next door, Alba Turchet. Alba came from a large Italian immigrant family, one of several who settled in Napa Junction. Pete's younger sister Helene also fell in love with a Turchet— Alba's younger brother Emory. When he turned twenty-one, Pete secured a liquor license and turned his father's corner store into a club. In 1956, he and Alba upgraded Pete's Club into a restaurant they called Palby's, a combination of both their names. At first there was just two dining rooms, a gift shop and the kitchen. The couple lived in a small house attached to the back of the restaurant.

This was no ordinary eatery. Family memorabilia filled the walls. Dolls were for sale in the gift shop. A Christmas village scene complete with miniature Ferris wheel went up in the winter of 1997 and was never put away. Palby's had a waterfall constructed by the Freskans, a trout pond, pony rides and an assortment of animals, most notably birds: peacocks, swans, doves, pigeons, silkie ducks and silver pheasants. For a while in the 1960s, Palby's had on display three sea lions that Pete captured and kept in a 100,000-gallon tank.

The menu was standard American-style cuisine: seafood, salads and steaks and what Palby's advertised as "deluxe western foods." A big slab of beef prime rib came with a tossed green salad, toasted cheese bread and the choice of a baked potato or buttered saffron rice. Much of the food was prepared by Jeannie McClenic, who worked at Palby's through most of its run. The daughter of Italian immigrants who settled in Napa Junction in the 1910s, she earned extra money babysitting for the Freskans. One night when the cook failed to turn up, Jeannie was pressed into service. At eight and a half months pregnant, she whipped up five hundred meals that night. She was so good, they kept her on.

Almost as soon as it opened, Palby's was popular. Professional, fraternal and religious organizations held their annual and monthly dinners there; local businesses hosted company parties; and political candidates shook hands and kissed babies. It was the go-to spot for someone looking to impress without breaking the bank. The food critic for the *Napa Register* in 1985 agreed:

> *When someone offers a steak dinner with all the trimmings for only $4.95, the wary diner usually starts thinking fine print of small portions. Neither is the case at Palby's Restaurant on the Napa Vallejo Highway....*
>
> *The famous 300-seat restaurant is both a treat to the palate and pocketbook. But the eager gourmet can look forward to more than just steak. The steak and lobster is succulent and filling, and the prime rib comes right from the Garden of Eden (jab, jab).*
>
> *The next time you head down to the Bay, or simply want to take a nice ride, include Palby's in your travel plans. One warning, you may have to wait a few minutes. Due to its popularity, Palby's is always busy, but it's well worth any short delay. While you're waiting, check out the funky gift shop; it's great!*

In 1981, some residents of American Canyon decided they wanted to incorporate as a city. One of the arguments made by those against it (including members of the Freskan clan) was that American Canyon was relatively crime-free and incorporation would lead to higher crime rates. What made this claim especially odd was that car accidents and crime—carjackings, kidnappings, robberies, burglaries, arson and so on—were

Lost Restaurants of Napa Valley and Their Recipes

A menu for the early bird specials at Palby's. *Courtesy of Rick Curry and the author.*

not unheard of at Napa Junction. Major incidents occurred at or near the restaurant at least once a year.

Even Pete ran afoul of the law. In 1960, he, a waitress and a bartender were sued by Arnie Patrick and Arlene Hodge for violating the Unruh Civil Rights Act, a California law passed in 1959 that banned discrimination based on "sex, race, color, religion, ancestry, national origin, disability, medical condition, genetic information, marital status, or sexual orientation." The complainants accused the waitress of setting out "reserved" signs on vacant tables and then telling the African American couple the wait was ninety minutes. When they went to the bar, the bartender ignored them. Arnie repeatedly asked for a drink until the bartender told him to "take the hint or you'll be smashed in the kisser." This was Napa County's first civil rights case post-Unruh, and the complainants hired a heavy-hitting attorney, Robert L. Leggett, then a candidate for state assembly. Pete countersued the couple for defamation and loss of business, but both cases were soon dismissed.

The push for incorporation in 1981 failed. It took another decade to get enough momentum to try again, but they finally succeeded. Not long after that, Palby's suffered an extensive fire. Sparks from the malfunctioning neon sign on the side of the building rapidly grew into twenty-foot flames. The higgledy-piggledy way the building had been added onto over the years made it difficult for firefighters to contain the fire. All told, the fire caused $70,000 in damages. Grateful diners were thrilled that the Freskans were able to rebuild enough of the structure to reopen within the week.

Mid-Century Modern

Once back at full capacity, the restaurant served five hundred meals a day—eight hundred to one thousand on weekends. Diners looking to save a few bucks had plenty of coupons to choose from. They changed frequently, offering rotating discounts on a lobster tail dinner, New York steak, fried prawns, the Four Corners Combo (Maine lobster tail, sirloin steak, grilled chicken breast and barbecue spare ribs), chicken fried steak, ranch steak, fish and chips, liver and onions, pasta Bolognese, brochettes kaulana (beef and chicken kabobs with green peppers, mushrooms and pineapple and served with rice) and roast turkey with stuffing, mashed potatoes and gravy. All those years of coupons and private banquets paid off when, in 1994, locals voted Palby's "the most economical restaurant for families."

By 2002, Pete, who had never fully recovered from a bad fall a few years back, and Alba were exhausted. Their sons John and Pierre and daughter-in-law Denise took over managing the restaurant while the elder Freskans took a backseat. Eventually the family decided it was time to close Palby's for good. One week later, Pete Freskan died. Then Vice Mayor of American Canyon Lori Luporini mourned the loss of Pete and Palby's, lamenting, "Everything was coming apart and it was like 46 years of history and basically the landmark for American Canyon."

Luporini was right: American Canyon was changing. Incorporation triggered a flood of construction. New housing projects brought in thousands of new residents, raising the population from just under six thousand in 1980 to almost twenty thousand in 2010. A massive shopping center colonized the land north of Palby's. Traffic crawled to a standstill as the little two-lane highway was suddenly packed with commuters, tourists and shoppers.

A couple of restaurateurs considered renovating Palby's, but the sales fell through. The site was turned into office space, and today it is the American Canyon Welcome Center. Palby's is gone, but it lives on in the hearts and minds of its regulars. "It was the place to be," wrote one local in loving tribute. "I will miss Palby's for a long time, if not forever."

Scalloped Potatoes and Wieners
Recipe provided to the *Napa Journal* by Maryellen De Lazzer, 1950

> Put 1 teaspoon oil in the pressure cooker. Add ½ cup milk, salt and pepper to taste. Cut potatoes (three medium sized ones serve two people) in thin slices and cover with sliced wieners. Bring to 15 pounds pressure for one minute. Then set to "OFF" and let pressure return to "DOWN."

Pork chops, ham slices, or sausage may be used instead of wieners. If sausage is used, cook first over a low heat to remove most of the grease. If pork chops are used, fry them brown first. Cooked ham may be used according to the wiener directions.

Venison Saute
Recipe provided to the *Napa Register* by Theresa Tamburelli, 1954

2 lbs. of boneless venison
1 cup dry mushrooms (soak in hot water, squeeze dry and chop; save liquid)
Chop together, using warm knife, 2 cloves garlic, 4 tablespoons onion, 1 thin slice salt pork, 4 tablespoons parsley
1 can solid pack tomatoes or 4 fresh tomatoes, chopped
¼ cup olive oil
2 tablespoons butter
¾ cup burgundy wine
1 red chili pepper (small and dry)
Spring rosemary

Sauté venison in hot oil and butter with chili and rosemary until well browned. Add chopped onion, parsley, mushrooms, garlic and salt pork and fry for a few minutes. Add wine and continue frying. Then add chopped tomatoes and liquid from mushrooms and salt. Simmer slowly for 1½ hours or until tender. Add more liquid during cooking process if necessary.

PART IX
RESTAURANT RENAISSANCE

THE 1950s AND 1960s WERE YEARS OF EXPANSION FOR NAPA COUNTY. The postwar population boom led to a rash of housing and business developments. At first, restaurants were slow to respond to the increase, but in the 1970s, a veritable cornucopia of dining options appeared. Fast-food chains and family-friendly sit-down restaurants clustered around shopping centers and major thoroughfares, while gourmet restaurants opened upvalley. There were two main reasons for the explosion of eateries: more locals eating out and more tourists coming into the valley. In 1980, the *Napa Register* estimated that while the population of the county was growing by 18 percent, the number of restaurants was increasing by 60 percent. For many families, it was easier and more economical to eat out than prepare meals at home.

At the dawn of the 1970s, most restaurants in Napa County were steakhouses, drive-ins, cafés, diners, inns and other family-friendly eateries with huge portions at miniscule prices. With the wine revival came the restaurant renaissance. Dishes from countless countries from nearly every continent were prepared by restaurateurs both American-born and immigrant. High-end restaurants generally stuck to French or Northern Italian or fiddled with fusion dishes. The rest featured American, Chinese and Mexican standards, plus new dishes from India, Thailand, Japan, Germany and elsewhere.

After Moet & Chandon opened Domaine Chandon and included a haute cuisine restaurant, other wineries quickly followed suit. Cooking classes, food pairings and personal chefs became fixtures in the wine industry. A new era of fine dining had begun, and Napa County cuisine would never be the same.

Chapter 24
Magnolia Hotel (Yountville)

Yountville got its name from George Yount, a South Carolinian mountain man who wandered into Napa Valley in the 1830s with hunter and blacksmith Guy Fling (or Flynn). Standing on the summit of Mount Saint Helena, George declared the valley the place he "would like to live and die." George got his wish. His friendship with General Mariano Vallejo was rewarded in 1836 when, after learning Spanish and converting to Catholicism, he was gifted a land grant—Rancho Caymus, named for the nearby Kaimus Wappo village. He holds the distinction of being the county's first American settler, first rancho owner, first winemaker and first vineyardist.

By and by came a school, church, post office and a few businesses. In 1865, the name was changed from Sebastopol (which already belonged to a town in Sonoma County) to Yountville. That same decade, the trans-county railway was completed, connecting Napa city to Calistoga and stopping at every township along the way. In 1870, five years after George's death, his heirs started selling off his property to eager developers like German immigrant Gottlob (sometimes spelled Gottlieb) Groezinger. Gottlob laid out ten blocks of roads and lots, planted two hundred acres of grapes, constructed a grand mansion for his family and built a huge brick cellar to store all his wine. The latter was later turned into a shopping and dining complex called Vintage 1870 and V Marketplace.

No one is quite sure who built the Magnolia Hotel. It was constructed from stone from a nearby quarry in the early 1870s. Dormers were added not long after that. The bricks for the addition were scavenged in the 1900s from the demolition of an old church, and the iron balcony came from the French Hospital in San Francisco. It is one of only three historic stone buildings left in Yountville. Not far from the train depot, the hotel and saloon were well positioned to take in travelers, as well as the area's agricultural laborers, field hands and vineyard workers needing a place to crash and something alcoholic to drink.

In the early 1900s, Pierre "Peter" Guillaume purchased the lot. Born in Spain, he immigrated to the United States in the late 1880s. Frances Lande, who had followed her older brother Dominic from France, won Peter's heart, and they married in 1890 at the Catholic church in St. Helena. He was a busy man. In St. Helena, he opened the German Bakery, then managed the Swiss Union Hotel and next the French Hotel. In 1895, the Guillaumes relocated to Yountville, where he ran the White House and the Eagle Hotel. He tried his luck in Pope Valley when he opened a four-cottage summer and winter resort in 1903 but was soon back in Yountville.

John Baptiste Lande, Frances's younger brother, managed the Magnolia during their Pope Valley sojourn. After joining his siblings in California, John lived all over the Bay Area before moving to Yountville in 1903 with his wife, Madeline. After a time, John switched occupations from saloonkeeper to steam laundry operator. He moved his business into a structure Peter had built in the early 1900s where he worked for many years. By the early 1910s, Peter was in control of the Magnolia once again.

Violating liquor laws seemed to have been an unofficial pastime of Peter's. While running the Eagle Hotel, he was accused of selling liquor during an election. A 1911 raid in Yountville netted ten arrests, including Peter, who pleaded not guilty. He was arrested two years later and again during Prohibition in 1920 when the sheriff "caught five men lined up at the Magnolia's bar with five drinks of wine before them, and the bartender with marked money in his hand, which he accepted in payment for the drinks." This time instead of a fine, Peter risked jail time for breaking a federal law. District Attorney Clarence Riggins threatened to shut down the hotel under the pretense that it was "a public nuisance." Judge Percy King determined that Peter had not sold alcohol in the hotel but in an attached building. The hotel was spared, but the smaller structure, converted after his arrest from a "soft drink house" to a rooming house, was closed for a year; Peter was forbidden from selling any more liquor in it and paid a $500 bond.

An illness claimed Peter's life in the spring of 1935, and a few months after that, Fred Marsh took over as proprietor. This marked the beginning

Restaurant Renaissance

Peter Guillaume may have painted the rates on an exterior wall: rooms were one dollar a day and meals twenty-five cents. Photograph taken July 1954. *Courtesy of Napa County Historical Society.*

of the end. In April 1936, Spanish-American War veteran Verdes Herron died in his room, likely from the effects of alcoholism. Napa County health officer Dr. Robert Northrop found the building in need of extensive repairs and wholly unfit for human occupancy. In lieu of boarding up the building, Peter's heirs granted a free, extended lease to the Yountville 4-H Club. Members made improvements during their stay, but after they left in 1950, the building fell into disrepair.

For years, the Magnolia sat forgotten and ignored, until Nancy and Ray Monte swooped in. As a child, Nancy had attended 4-H meetings in the hotel, and it pained her to see it in such a state. They poured time, money and effort into the restoration so that by 1971 it was once again ready to take in guests. In 1973, the Montes added a restaurant. Chef Conrad "Pancho" Caseres created a menu of soup, petit beef Wellington, poached halibut with lobster sauce, roast lamb with mushroom sauce, roast duckling and veal cordon bleu. They planned to serve fifty family-style dinners a night, Wednesday through Sunday. But a few days before the scheduled opening, the city declared the building unsafe because of a permitting issue. It took four years, but in the spring of 1977, the Montes finally opened their

Above: Undated photo of the Magnolia Hotel. *Courtesy of Napa County Historical Society.*

Left: The Magnolia Hotel in August 1977, a few months before the Lockens purchased it. Photographer Judith Munns. *Courtesy of Napa County Historical Society.*

restaurant, this time under the guidance of a French chef. They sold the business not long after that.

Bruce and Bonnie Locken took what the Montes started and elevated it. Bonnie was a registered dietician for a chain of hospitals, while Bruce spent most of his career as a general manager of pricey hotels such as the Clift Hotel in San Francisco, the Cabana Hyatt Hotel in Palo Alto and the Casa Munras in Monterey. With Bonnie in the kitchen, Bruce managing the business and wine supply and acting as maître d' and their sons Craig and Lars as waiters, dishwashers and busboys, the Lockens had a hand in every aspect of the hotel.

For seven years, the Magnolia served a five-course dinner four nights a week. There were entrées of pork or lamb on Thursdays, seafood on Fridays, beef on Saturdays and poultry on Sundays. For dessert, guests had their choice of chocolate mousse, chocolate rum pie or Magnolia Hotel Pie (Bonnie's take on baked Alaska). The pâté first course was usually prepared by Bruce, but everything else was all Bonnie. Bonnie favored French cuisine, but sometimes she experimented with chicken paprikash, Viennese roast loin of pork or other European dishes. Dinner was open to the public, but breakfast was for hotel guests only. Besides the usual fare of oatmeal, cereal, fresh fruit, juice, tea and coffee, diners sampled the sheepherder's bread French toast with port wine syrup; shirred eggs; an omelet with sherry, mushrooms and cheese; and thick-cut bacon and sausage.

Although Bonnie was not a professionally trained chef, she had a natural gift, as her son Craig Graffin fondly remembered. Chef Julia Child enjoyed her meal there so much she wrote Bonnie a note praising her savvy in the kitchen. Just getting into the restaurant was a bit of a challenge for Julia. The door was lower than usual, and because she was so tall, she had to stoop to enter. She was not the only celebrity to grace the Magnolia's halls; others included George Lucas, Peter Gallagher, Vidal Sassoon, Shaun Cassidy and television stars Donna Mills, Morgan Woodward and Alex Trebek.

The Magnolia Hotel was at the forefront of what would become a wave of gourmet restaurants. As pricier dining experiences and luxury hotels gained a foothold in the county, more and more people were opting for weekend excursions instead of afternoon trips. Word of mouth was all the Lockens needed to maintain a steady stream of visitors. With its antique Victorian decor, marble-topped vanities, twenty-by-forty-foot swimming pool, sunken hot tub and huge brass beds, guests often came year after year. The excellent wine collection did not hurt, either. Bruce had extensive contacts in the industry, many of whom hand-delivered cases of wines not readily available

The Lockens encouraged the ivy to cover the stone and brick walls. Photograph taken in the 1980s. *Courtesy of Craig Graffin.*

Restaurant Renaissance

The breakfast room, May 1983. *Courtesy of Craig Graffin.*

The Magnolia's longtime receptionist LaRee Gawley worked on this piece on her downtime and completed it in 1981. *Courtesy of Craig Graffin and the author.*

in stores. The 1970 Heitz Cellar Martha's Vineyard Cabernet Sauvignon, 1973 Stags' Leap Petite Sirah and 1978 Grgich Hills Chardonnay topped a list of nearly three hundred fine wines.

In 1984, the demands of running both the hotel and restaurant proved too great. The Lockens ended dinner service but continued serving breakfast. By that point, visitors had a bounty of new fine dining restaurants to select from. The hotel lasted until 1993, when Bruce passed away. The family sold the business and property but remained in the county. Not long after that, Chef Thomas Keller took over the restaurant the French Laundry (so named because of the French laundry operator who owned it, John Lande), turning the quaint town of Yountville into a hub for haute cuisine. Today, the Magnolia Hotel is the home of the Maison Fleurie Inn.

For foodies, the restaurant boom was heaven on earth. The Culinary Institute of America opened a branch of its premier cooking school and restaurant in the former Greystone Winery in the 1990s, and the French Laundry became one of the first Michelin-starred restaurants in the Napa Valley in the early 2000s. Yet some locals found it overwhelming. A Napan bemoaned in a letter to the editor of the *Napa Register* that restaurants were "taking over" the county. In 1980, Yountville, a town of fewer than three thousand people, had a dozen restaurants, including the Magnolia Hotel. A little while later, a Calistoga restaurateur complained the area was "saturated with restaurants."

Fine dining establishments glutted the upvalley region, but it took until the turn of the millennium for the trend to find sustained success in Napa city. The city had a few upscale places, such as the French restaurants Chanterelle and the Carriage House Restaurant. Many more suffered spectacular collapses—COPIA and its restaurant that paid homage to Julia Child, Budo and its overpriced Asian-Californian fare and many more. Hoss Zaré, owner of the Iranian-Californian cuisine restaurant Zaré, believed the failure of his own place in 2007 was caused by the slump in business during the winter and a large population of locals who had begun to eat out less often and spent less money when they did. When Greg Cole opened Celadon in 1996 and Cole's Chop House in 2000, the two fine dining restaurants kickstarted the downtown revitalization project to pull tourists off Highway 29 and onto Main Street. And when Oxbow Public Market opened in 2007, it kindled a new interest in world cuisine.

Now, two decades into the new millennium, locals and tourists alike relish the vast array of eateries available. Chop suey has slipped in favor, but oysters, tamales, malfatti, burgers and haute cuisine still hold sway. From the rough-and-tumble Empire Saloon to Mrs. Tobin's prim-and-proper restaurant to the five-course fanciness of both Magnolia Hotels, Napa County's tastes have changed as much as they have stayed the same. Since time immemorial, the people here have cherished the act of sharing food with those we care about. Whatever the future of our culinary culture may be, we will always hold on to our love of a good meal.

Spinach Pie (Spanakopeta)
Recipe provided to the *Napa Register* by Spiros Drossos, owner of and cook at Speero's, 1989

2 bunches scallions, chopped, including some green tops
1 bunch leeks, white only, chopped
¼ cup of extra virgin olive oil
8 eggs beaten
3 bunches spinach, washed drained and chopped
1 pound Feta cheese
1 bunch parsley, finely chopped
Dash of dill
2 mint leaves, finely chopped
White pepper, scant
½ pound butter, melted
½ cup olive oil
½ pound phyllo pastry

Sauté scallions and leeks in olive oil. Beat eggs slightly; add spinach, cheese, sauteed scallions and leeks, parsley, dill, mint and white pepper. Add salt if needed and set aside. Combine oil with melted butter and brush 17 by 12 by 2 inch pan generously. Layer 4 sheets phyllo pastry, brushing well between each sheet with oil-butter mixture, leaving 3 or 4 sheets phyllo hanging over each side. Pour in spinach mixture and bring up phyllo hanging over sides. Add remaining phyllo, brushing each sheet well with oil-butter mixture.

Butter top sheet and with sharp knife, score top layers of phyllo making sure you do not go through to the spinach mixture. Bake in 350 degree oven for 1 hour. When slightly cool cut all the way through. Size of squares depends upon how many you intend to serve.

Salmon with Smoked, Sun-Dried Tomatoes and Roasted Corn on Cilantro Pistou

Recipe provided to the *Napa Register* by Chef Hervé Glin of Starmont Restaurant, 1989

4 6-ounce slices of salmon
1 tablespoon sea salt
½ cup sun-dried tomato halves
¾ cup corn cut from cob
¾ cup chopped red onions

For Cilantro Pistou

1 bunch cilantro leaves
2 cloves garlic
¼ cup parmesan cheese
¼ cup pine nuts
1 cup olive oil
Juice of ½ lemon
Salt and pepper to taste

Pistou & Tomatoes: Blend garlic, pine nuts, cilantro and parmesan cheese together. Add olive oil slowly with lemon juice. Smoke the sun-dried tomatoes on barbecue at low heat for ten minutes. Let cool and dice. Keep two tablespoons of oil for tomato marinade. Sauté corn and onion in non-adhesive pan and add sun-dried tomatoes. Bring to boil for a moment. Set aside. Finish with chopped cilantro leaves.

Cooking salmon: Sauté salmon in non-adhesive pan or on grill. Season lightly after removing from heat.

Plating: Spread 2 tablespoons of pistou in center of plate. Place salmon on the pistou and finish with mix of corn, sun-dried tomatoes and red onions just covering the salmon (2 tablespoons).

Note: You can serve with asparagus tips, approximately 5 on each plate.

Sprinkle some grated parmesan around salmon.

Serves 4.

Bibliography

PART I. THE EARLY DAYS OF EATING OUT

Bancroft, Hubert Howe. "Drinking." *The Works of Hubert Howe Bancroft: California Inter Pocula*. Vol. 35. San Francisco: History Company, 1888. archive.org/details/bwcalinterpoc35bancroft.

"Menus: The Art of Dining." University of Nevada Las Vegas Digital Collections. 2018. digital.library.unlv.edu/collections/menus.

Sprang, Rebecca L. *The Invention of the Restaurant: Paris and Modern Gastronomic Culture*. Cambridge, MA: Harvard University Press, 2000.

Empire Saloon

Hoover, Mildred Brooke, Hero Eugene Rensch, Ethel Grace Rensch and William N. Abeloe. *Historic Spots in California*. 5th ed. Revised by Douglas E. Kyle. Stanford, CA: Stanford University Press, 2002.

Kanaga, Tillie, and W.F. Wallace. *History of Napa County*. Oakland, CA: Enquirer Print, 1901.

Menefee, C.A. *Historical and Descriptive Sketch Book of Napa, Sonoma, Lake, and Mendocino*. Napa, CA: Reporter Publishing House, 1873.

Napa Reporter. "Napa City." December 15, 1890. Napa County Newspaper Archive.

BIBLIOGRAPHY

Dorr's Saloons

Bancroft, "Drinking."
Dickson, Paul. "The Great American Ice Cream Book." *Newsweek Condensed Books*. Edited by Kermit Lansner, 6–55. New York: Newsweek, Inc., 1973. archive.org/details/newsweekbooks00news.
Menefee, *Historical and Descriptive Sketch Book of Napa*.
Napa County Reporter. "Achille Monmert…" April 11, 1868. Napa County Newspaper Archive.
———. "Blumer's Saloon." March 30, 1861. Huntington Library.
———. "Blumer's Saloon." September 6, 1862. California State Library.
———. "Capitol Saloon." May 7, 1864. Napa County Newspaper Archive.
———. "Fashion Saloon." January 2, 1864. Napa County Newspaper Archive.
———. "New Liquor Store." June 11, 1864. Napa County Newspaper Archive.
———. "Paris Restaurant." August 7, 1869. Napa County Newspaper Archive.
———. "Statistics of Napa City." March 30, 1861. Huntington Library.
Napa Register. "Paris Restaurant." February 19, 1870. California State Library.
———. "We Are Glad to Notice…" May 23, 1874. Napa County Newspaper Archive.
Turner, Katherine Leonard. *How the Other Half Ate: A History of Working-Class Meals at the Turn of the Century*. Berkeley: University of California Press, 2014.

Valley House Restaurant

Menefee, *Historical and Descriptive Sketch Book of Napa*.
Napa County Reporter. "Valley House Restaurant." August 29, 1857. California State Library.
Napa Journal. "One of Napa's Old Pioneers Passed Away." May 16, 1915. Napa County Newspaper Archive.
Pacific Echo. "Cheap Living." November 8, 1862. St. Helena Public Library.
———. "Dinner for the Fourth at the Valley Rsetaurant [*sic*]." July 4, 1862. St. Helena Public Library.
———. "Valley House Restaurant!" October 18, 1862. St. Helena Public Library.

BIBLIOGRAPHY

PART II. "THE LUSCIOUS BIVALVE"

Napa County Reporter. "Arcade Saloon." November 14, 1863. Napa County Newspaper Archive.

Napa Register. "A. Javon." March 21, 1879. Napa County Newspaper Archive.

St. Helena Star. "The 'Elite.'" October 4, 1889. Napa County Newspaper Archive.

———. "The Luscious Bivalve." December 8, 1876. Napa County Newspaper Archive.

———. "Railroad House." December 3, 1874. Napa County Newspaper Archive.

Arcade Restaurant

Lobel, Cindy R. "'Out to Eat': The Emergence and Evolution of the Restaurant in Nineteenth-Century New York." *Winterthur Portfolio* 44, no. 2/3 (Summer/Autumn 2010): 193–220. JSTOR. www.jstor.org/stable/10.1086/654885.

Napa County Reporter. "Arcade Redivus." September 20, 1873. California State Library.

———. "Arcade Restaurant." September 6, 1862. California State Library.

———. "Arcade Restaurant." May 25, 1872. California State Library.

———. "Arcade Restaurant." July 6, 1872. California State Library.

———. "Arcade Restaurant." July 22, 1887. Napa County Newspaper Archive.

———. "As We Journey Through Life, Let Us Live on the Way." "Arcade Restaurant." May 11, 1872. California State Library.

———. "$10,000 Blaze." July 6, 1884. Napa County Newspaper Archive.

Napa Journal. "James Ritchie Leaves This Afternoon…" March 3, 1887. Napa County Newspaper Archive.

———. "J.C. Ritchie's 'Fountain Restaurant.'" May 25, 1890. Napa County Newspaper Archive.

Napa Register. "J.F. Schwartz…" March 1, 1895. Napa County Newspaper Archive.

———. "Mrs. M. T. Pickle…" July 8, 1892. Napa County Newspaper Archive.

———. "This Is Opening Day at the Fountain Restaurant…" August 19, 1887. Napa County Newspaper Archive.

Bibliography

———. "Two Failures." June 10, 1892. Napa County Newspaper Archive.

Ruffin, Herbert G., II. "The Conventions of Colored Citizens of the State of California (1855–1865)." *BlackPast*. February 4, 2009. www.blackpast.org/african-american-history/conventions-colored-citizens-state-california-1855-1865.

The Nielsens' Restaurants

"The Coffee Saloon Idea." *The Tea and Coffee Trade Journal* 36, no. 4. (April 1919): 325–26. books.google.com/books?id=eU1Gl34FIbcC.

Cowan, Brian. *The Social Life of Coffee: The Emergence of the British Coffeehouse*. New Haven, CT: Yale University Press, 2005.

Hattox, Ralph S. *Coffee and Coffeehouses: The Origins of a Social Beverage in the Medieval Near East*. Seattle: University of Washington Press, 1996.

St. Helena Star. "Another Business Change." May 24, 1895. Napa County Newspaper Archive.

———. "John Nielsen Is Having His Restaurant…" March 18, 1887. Napa County Newspaper Archive.

———. "John Nielsen, of the St. Helena Restaurant…" December 3, 1874. Napa County Newspaper Archive.

———. "Nielsen's Restaurant." February 9, 1894. Napa County Newspaper Archive.

———. "Paul Neunkirsch…" February 21, 1896. Napa County Newspaper Archive.

———. "St. Helena Restaurant and Coffee Saloon." September 24, 1886. Napa County Newspaper Archive.

———. "Took His Own Life." February 21, 1896. Napa County Newspaper Archive.

Trobits, Monika. *Bay Area Coffee: A Stimulating History*. Charleston, SC: The History Press, 2019.

Ukhers, William H. "History of Coffee Propagation." *All About Coffee*. New York: The Tea and Coffee Trade Journal Company, 1922. archive.org/details/allaboutcoffee00ukeruoft.

BIBLIOGRAPHY

PART III. ROOM AND BOARD

Fellows, Charles. *The Menu Maker.* Chicago: Hotel Monthly, 1910. books.google.com/books?id=XbQv2SNlbNEC.

Melendy, Royal L. "The Saloon in Chicago." *American Journal of Sociology* 6, no. 4 (January 1901): 433–64. JSTOR. www.jstor.org/stable/2762287.

Menefee, *Historical and Descriptive Sketch Book of Napa.*

Munns, Judith. "Suscol House." National Register of Historic Places Nomination Form (Washington, D.C.: U.S. Department of the Interior, National Park Service, 1978), Sections 7–8. npgallery.nps.gov/GetAsset/baa29544-f92b-41ad-bd3b-a185da5de9cd.

Napa County Reporter. "American House." October 11, 1862. Huntington Library.

———. "Restaurant 'Plans.'" February 28, 1863. Huntington Library

Napa Weekly Reporter. "American House." November 12, 1866. Napa County Newspaper Archive.

Pacific Echo. "Eating and Sleeping." January 24, 1863. St. Helena Public Library.

Tellman, John. *The Practical Hotel Steward: Revised to Incorporate Both American & European Plans.* 4th ed. Chicago: Hotel Monthly, 1913. books.google.com/books?id=XTkEAAAAYAAJ.

Exchange and French Restaurants

Napa County Reporter. "Exchange Restaurant!" February 9, 1861. Huntington Library.

———. "Exchange Restaurant." June 22, 1861. Huntington Library.

———. "For Sale or Lease." June 21, 1878. California State Library.

———. "French Restaurant." June 28, 1862. Napa County Newspaper Archive.

———. "French Restaurant." September 6, 1862. Huntington Library.

———. "On the American Plan." March 14, 1863. Huntington Library.

Napa Register. "Choice of the Market and Fat of the Land at the French Restaurant." February 19, 1870. California State Library.

Pacific Echo. "Hurrah for the 4th of July!" July 4, 1862. St. Helena Public Library.

———. "Notice to the Public." January 10, 1863. St. Helena Public Library.

———. "Partnership Notice." June 28, 1862. St. Helena Public Library.

Bibliography

Napa Hotel

Napa County Reporter. "Christmas Dinner." December 20, 1862. Huntington Library.

———. "Disastrous Conflagration." November 21, 1884. Napa County Newspaper Archive.

———. "A Fine Structure." February 20, 1885. Napa County Newspaper Archive.

———. "Ice Cream." April 19, 1862. Huntington Library.

———. "Look Out for Paint." March 28, 1867. Napa County Newspaper Archive.

———. "Napa Hotel." January 16, 1885. Napa County Newspaper Archive.

———. "The Napa Hotel." June 19, 1885. Napa County Newspaper Archive.

———. "Napa House." December 27, 1862. Huntington Library.

———. "Napa Restaurant." September 14, 1861. Huntington Library.

———. "Napa Restaurant." March 29, 1862. Huntington Library.

———. "New Cook Range." January 4, 1873. California State Library.

———. "Piscatorial." May 6, 1871. California State Library.

———. "Plans for the New Napa Hotel." October 17, 1874. California State Library.

Napa Journal. "For Those Good Eats." February 20, 1926. Napa County Newspaper Archive.

———. "Mrs. Hawley…" August 11, 1897. Napa County Newspaper Archive.

———. "Napa Delicatessen." January 23, 1926. Napa County Newspaper Archive.

———. "Napa Delicatessen Open for Business." July 17, 1925. Napa County Newspaper Archive.

———. "The Napa Hotel." December 24, 1898. Napa County Newspaper Archive.

———. "A New Grill Room." June 29, 1897. Napa County Newspaper Archive.

———. "The Proprietor of the Napa Hotel…" October 1, 1892. Napa County Newspaper Archive.

Napa Register. "Approaching Completion." April 24, 1885. Napa County Newspaper Archive.

———. "Napa Hotel Dining Room." November 29, 1926. Napa County Newspaper Archive.

Bibliography

———. "Napa Hotel Dinner Bill of Fare." September 16, 1871. California State Library.

———. "Under New Management." February 16, 1923. Napa County Newspaper Archive.

Pacific Echo. "Hot Egg Muffins and American Waffles…" July 12, 1862. St. Helena Public Library.

———. "Napa Restaurant!" June 28, 1862. St. Helena Public Library.

Magnolia Hotel (Calistoga)

Bazolli, Kathy, and Kent Domogalla. "Take a Walk Down Lincoln Avenue's Past." *Calistogan.* February 25, 2015. www.napavalleyregister.com.

Independent Calistogian. "Calistoga Scorched!" August 19, 1885. Napa County Newspaper Archive.

———. "The Chesebro Property…" February 12, 1897. Napa County Newspaper Archive.

———. "J.A. Chesebro, Proprietor…" January 2, 1878. Napa County Newspaper Archive.

———. "The Magnolia Hotel…" December 18, 1889. Napa County Newspaper Archive.

———. "The Masquerade Ball." February 27, 1889. Napa County Newspaper Archive.

———. "New Year's Eve Ball." January 2, 1878. Napa County Newspaper Archive.

———. "The Red Rooster." March 6, 1889. Napa County Newspaper Archive.

———. "The Remains of J.E. Nichols…" May 15, 1889. Napa County Newspaper Archive.

Napa Daily Reporter. "J.A. Chesebro Has Run…" November 22, 1878. Napa County Newspaper Archive.

Napa Journal. "Calistoga News." December 19, 1892. Napa County Newspaper Archive.

———. "Chesebro Received…" December 7, 1872. Napa County Newspaper Archive.

———. "Fire at Calistoga." June 19, 1890. Napa County Newspaper Archive.

———. "The Good People of Calistoga…" September 9, 1899. Napa County Newspaper Archive.

San Francisco Call. "Fierce Fire Makes Ruin of Calistoga." August 3, 1901. California Digital Newspaper Collection.

St. Helena Star. "Dropped Dead." November 10, 1893. Napa County Newspaper Archive.

Aetna Springs Resort

Callizo, Joe. "Pope Valley Memories: The Stories of Joe Callizo, an Oral History." *Napa Register*, March 31, 2012. Napa County Newspaper Archive.

Eberling, Barry. "Napa County's Famed Aetna Springs Has New Owner with Resort Plans." *Napa Register*, December 20, 2018. Napa County Newspaper Archive.

Ruvoli, JoAnne. "Frances Marion." In *Women Film Pioneers Project*. Edited by Jane Gaines, Radha Vatsal and Monica Dall'Asta. New York: Columbia University Libraries, September 27, 2013. wfpp.cdrs.columbia.edu/pioneer/ccp-frances-marion.

Shinnamon, Felicia. "Aetna Springs Memories." *Napa Register*, August 3, 2014. Napa County Newspaper Archive.

St. Helena Star. "New Club House at Aetnas." May 28, 1909. Napa County Newspaper Archive.

Woodbridge, Sally B. "Aetna Springs Resort." National Register of Historic Places Nomination Form (Washington, D.C.: U.S. Department of the Interior, National Park Service, 1987), Sections 7–8. npgallery.nps.gov/GetAsset/f6892286-6e5a-4fa6-b4e8-d013c39e6ae1.

PART IV. CHILI QUEENS AND TAMALE MEN

Heidenreich, Linda. *"This Land Was Mexican Once": Histories of Resistance from Northern California*. Austin: University of Texas Press, 2007.

"Land Use—Native American History." McLaughlin Natural Reserve. Last modified February 5, 2009. nrs.ucdavis.edu/mcl/natural/land/native.html.

Menefee, *Historical and Descriptive Sketch Book of Napa*.

Ridpath, John Clark. "Beyond the Sierras: A Tour of Sixty Days Through the Valleys of California." In *Transactions of the American Horticultural Society, for the Year 1888*. Vol. 5. Comp. W.H. Ragan. Indianapolis: Carlon & Hollenbeck, 1888. books.google.com/books?id=RAVJAAAAMAAJ.

BIBLIOGRAPHY

Rose, Viviene Juarez. *The Past Is Father of the Present: Spanish California History and Family Legends, 1737–1973, San Francisco and Napa County.* Vallejo, CA: Wheeler Printing, Inc., 1974.

Stewart, Omer C. *Forgotten Fires: Native Americans and the Transient Wilderness.* Norman: University of Oklahoma Press, 2002.

St. Helena Star. "Mr. B. Bruck…" September 11, 1896. Napa County Newspaper Archive.

Tamale Parlors

Independent Calistogian. "St. Helena's Harvest Festival." November 19, 1897. Napa County Newspaper Archive.

Napa Journal. "The Genuine Garcia…" October 2, 1897. Napa County Newspaper Archive.

———. "Hunter's Fruit Depot…" February 19, 1897. Napa County Newspaper Archive.

———. "J. Higuera Passes Away." October 9, 1934. Napa County Newspaper Archive.

———. "Napa Cafe." September 9, 1897. Napa County Newspaper Archive.

———. "Spanish-American Chop House." November 12, 1897. Napa County Newspaper Archive.

———. "Tomales for Sale." October 1, 1893. Napa County Newspaper Archive.

———. "Two Are Naturalized." August 3, 1906. Napa County Newspaper Archive.

Napa Register. "Good Home-Made Tomales." February 15, 1923. Napa County Newspaper Archive.

———. "Imperial Tamale Parlor." September 22, 1923. Napa County Newspaper Archive.

———. "Mrs. W.H. Olds Passes Away." April 19, 1926. Napa County Newspaper Archive.

———. "Napa Couple Journeyed to Reno to Wed." February 27, 1928. Napa County Newspaper Archive.

T.D.S. "Jilted." *Napa Journal*, October 10, 1902. Napa County Newspaper Archive.

BIBLIOGRAPHY

Dabner Brothers Restaurant

Napa Journal. "Go to Dabner Bros & Co." February 1, 1896. Napa County Newspaper Archive
———. "New Restaurant." April 7, 1900. Napa County Newspaper Archive.
Simons, Cynthia Vrilakas. *San Leandro.* Charleston, SC: Arcadia Publishing, 2008.
Wilson, Simone. *Petaluma.* Charleston, SC: Arcadia Publishing, 2001.

Spanish Restaurant

Ezettie, Louis. "Looking into Napa's Past and Present." *Napa Register,* November 12, 1969. Napa County Newspaper Archive.
———. "Looking into Napa's Past and Present." *Napa Register,* March 25, 1972. Napa County Newspaper Archive.
Napa Journal. "Beef and Chicken Tamales." March 27, 1928. Napa County Newspaper Archive.
———. "Ed Quijado to Retire After 37 Years in Business in This City." February 22, 1935. Napa County Newspaper Archive.
———. "Ordinance No. 560." April 3, 1917. Napa County Newspaper Archive.
———. "Raid on Redlight." November 15, 1913. Napa County Newspaper Archive.
———. "Sam Boyd's Appetite." February 24, 1901. Napa County Newspaper Archive.
———. "Sam Boyd's Appetite." October 26, 1901. Napa County Newspaper Archive.
———. "Twenty Years Ago." May 3, 1930. Napa County Newspaper Archive.
Napa Register. "Around Town with the Rounder." April 11, 1936. Napa County Newspaper Archive.
———. "Ed Quijada, 83, Pioneer, Passes." January 30, 1956. Napa County Newspaper Archive.
———. "Mrs Ed. Quijada Succumbs." December 20, 1937. Napa County Newspaper Archive.
———. "No New City Hall." April 22, 1908. Napa County Newspaper Archive.

BIBLIOGRAPHY

———. "Samuel Boyd, Resident of Napa County Since 1876, Passes Away." July 23, 1926. Napa County Newspaper Archive.
———. "This Is a Fact." July 22, 1892. Napa County Newspaper Archive.

El Faro Restaurant

Calistogan. "Christmas Program at Community Church." December 23, 1971. Napa County Newspaper Archive.
———. "El Faro Mexican Restaurant." February 24, 1983. Napa County Newspaper Archive.
———. "El Faro Restaurant Now Open." June 10, 1971. Napa County Newspaper Archive.
Huffman, Jennifer. "Napa's Compadres Restaurant to Close Feb. 18." *Napa Register*, February 8, 2019. Napa County Newspaper Archive.
Napa Register. "Greg Hernandez." February 11, 1996. Napa County Newspaper Archive.
St. Helena Star. "El Faro Restaurant." October 28, 1982. Napa County Newspaper Archive.
———. "Now Open El Cafe Talpita…" May 2, 1963 Napa County Newspaper Archive.

PART V. CHOW CHOP SUEY

Freedman, Paul. *Ten Restaurants that Changed America.* New York: Liveright Publishing, 2016.
Liu, Haiming. *From Canton Restaurant to Panda Express: A History of Chinese Food in the United States.* New Brunswick, NJ: Rutgers University Press, 2015.

Lai Hing Company

Napa Register. "The Chinese New Year." February 8, 1889. Napa County Newspaper Archive.
Wong, H.K. *Gum Sahn Yun: Gold Mountain Men.* San Francisco: Bechtel Publications, 1987.

BIBLIOGRAPHY

Sang Wo's Lunch Counter

Napa Journal. "Russ House Grill." February 9, 1912. Napa County Newspaper Archive.

———. "Sang Wo's Lunch Counter." May 27, 1915. Napa County Newspaper Archive.

———. "Vallejo Saloons." March 22, 1907. Napa County Newspaper Archive.

———. "When You Want Something Good to Eat…" June 16, 1909. Napa County Newspaper Archive.

Napa Register. "'Dry' Case Has Been Dismissed." October 20, 1922. Napa County Newspaper Archive.

Palmatier, Robert A. *Food: A Dictionary of Literal and Nonliteral Terms*. Westport, CT: Greenwood Press, 2000.

A-1 Cafe

Calistogan. "A-1 Cafe." May 24, 1956. Napa County Newspaper Archive.

———. "Looking Back Through the Pages of 1984." December 28, 1984. Napa County Newspaper Archive.

———. "Wong's Open New Plus Restaurant." August 12, 1976. Napa County Newspaper Archive.

Liu, *From Canton Restaurant to Panda Express*.

Napa Journal. "Just Good Food." June 26, 1942. Napa County Newspaper Archive.

Napa Register. "Albert Lee." October 13, 1994. Napa County Newspaper Archive.

———. "A-1 Cafe Will Open Tomorrow." June 22, 1934. Napa County Newspaper Archive.

———. "Bing Soon." December 1, 2000. Napa County Newspaper Archive.

———. "Chinese Foods." September 3, 1965. Napa County Newspaper Archive.

———. "Henry Owyeong." July 11, 1989. Napa County Newspaper Archive.

———. "Napa Hotel Dining Room." November 29, 1926. Napa County Newspaper Archive.

———. "Open Saturday…" June 22, 1934. Napa County Newspaper Archive.

---. "Soft Drink Parlor." July 22, 1921. Napa County Newspaper Archive.

---. "Wong's Restaurant Moves to New Trancas Location." August 15, 1976. Napa County Newspaper Archive.

Soon, Herman. Interview by Alexandria Brown. July 6, 2019.

St. Helena Star. "A-1 Cafe." February 19, 1959. Napa County Newspaper Archive.

---. "New Chinese Restaurant Offers Mandarin Cuisine." May 18, 1985. Napa County Newspaper Archive.

Villano, Matt. "2013: Celebrating 10 Years Since Renovation and Re-Opening." *Napa Valley Opera House.* www.nvoh.org/history-1.

PART VI. LITTLE ITALY

Baccari, Alessandro. "The Italians Who Shaped California." In *Cerca di una Nuova Vita: Italy to California, Italian Immigration: 1850 to Today.* N.p., 2009.

Calistogan. "Ruffino's." June 25, 1964. Napa County Newspaper Archive.

Di Franco, J. Philip. *The Italian Americans.* New York: Chelsea House Publishers, 1988.

Undated advertisement for Alfredo's House of Pizza from an unknown newspaper. Restaurant File. Ephemera File. Napa County Historical Society, Napa, California.

The Depot

Callan, John L. "The Tornari Sisters: Virginia Ferrogiaro, Catarina Carbone, and Maria Luchetti, Napa Italian Pioneers." MS 218 2015.48. Napa County Historical Society.

Carson, L. Pierce. "Napa Tradition to Continue at the Depot." *Napa Register*, September 7, 2004. Napa County Newspaper Archive.

Courtney, Kevin. "Waving Goodbye to Ferro Glove." *Napa Register*, December 2, 2009. Napa County Newspaper Archive.

Coverdale, Jennifer. "Discovering Italian Roots in Wine Country." *Napa Register*, September 4, 1995. Napa County Newspaper Archive.

Ezettie, Louis. "Looking into Napa's Past and Present." *Napa Register*, October 11, 1967. Napa County Newspaper Archive.

BIBLIOGRAPHY

Frazer, Margaret. "The Depot Hotel: Italian Dining for the Penny-wise and the Pound-foolish." *Napa Valley Magazine*, October 1979.

Morehouse, Lisa. "Malfatti, the Dumpling that Became a Napa Valley Legend." NPR, October 8, 2016. www.npr.org.

Napa Journal. "Depot Hotel." January 15, 1927. Napa County Newspaper Archive.

———. "His Aim Was Poor." November 2, 1894. Napa County Newspaper Archive.

———. "His Preliminary Examination." November 2, 1894. Napa County Newspaper Archive.

———. "Napa Valley Inn." October 1, 1936. Napa County Newspaper Archive.

———. "Tamburelli Is Freed by Commissioner James Palmer." September 9, 1930. Napa County Newspaper Archive.

Napa Register. "Angelina Momsen." May 15, 2003. Napa County Newspaper Archive.

———. "Batista J. Tamburelli." December 26, 1973. Napa County Newspaper Archive.

———. "The Depot Adds Outdoor Dining." May 31, 2005. Napa County Newspaper Archive.

———. "The Depot Hotel: Now That's Italian!" March 10, 1997. Napa County Newspaper Archive.

———. "Malfatti Queen." February 20, 1954. Napa County Newspaper Archive.

———. "Napa Still Case Opens in Court." January 13, 1931. Napa County Newspaper Archive.

———. "N. Tamburelli Now Owns Depot Hotel." December 23, 1935. Napa County Newspaper Archive.

———. "Rites Set for J. Tamburelli." November 18, 1937. Napa County Newspaper Archive.

———. "Theresa Tamburelli." July 8, 1971. Napa County Newspaper Archive.

Renfrew, J.M. "Archaeology and the Origins of Wine Production." In *Wine: A Scientific Exploration*, edited by Merton Sandler and Roger Pinder, 56–68. New York: Taylor & Francis, 2003.

Rose, *Past Is Father of the Present*.

Sams, Reid. "Years Change Depot Hotel Very Little." *Napa Register*, July 23, 1987. Napa County Newspaper Archive.

St. Helena Star. "Real Home Cooking." August 31, 1934. Napa County Newspaper Archive.

BIBLIOGRAPHY

USGS. "The Great 1906 San Francisco Earthquake." earthquake.usgs.gov/earthquakes/events/1906calif/18april.
Weber, Lin. *Roots of the Present: Napa Valley 1900–1950.* St. Helena, CA: Wine Ventures Publishing, 2001.
Zeller, Robert. Interview by Alexandria Brown. August 7, 2019.

Napa Raviola and Noodle Parlor

Napa Journal. "Are You Looking for Advertising Results?" February 16, 1933. Napa County Newspaper Archive.
———. "$500 Fire Damage to Stores in Napa Hotel Building." February 13, 1929. Napa County Newspaper Archive.
———. "For Those Good Eats." February 20, 1926. Napa County Newspaper Archive.
———. "Louis Zaro Buys Store." January 8, 1927. Napa County Newspaper Archive.
———. "Napa Delicatessen." January 23, 1926. Napa County Newspaper Archive.
———. "25 Federal Officers Take Part in Liquor Raids Here Yesterday." September 9, 1932. Napa County Newspaper Archive.
Napa Register. "Ex-Patient Jailed on Check Count." August 30, 1933. Napa County Newspaper Archive.
———. "In Conjunction." July 21, 1930. Napa County Newspaper Archive.
———. "Miss Sipkins Elected Queen." September 26, 1928. Napa County Newspaper Archive.
———. "Napa Man Appears in Police Court." August 26, 1933. Napa County Newspaper Archive.

PART VII. EARLY TWENTIETH-CENTURY CLASSICS

Frey, William H. "The New Great Migration: Black Americans' Return to the South, 1965–2000." www.brookings.edu/research/the-new-great-migration-black-americans-return-to-the-south-1965-2000.
Napa Journal. "C.M. Kitoka and J. Nankagawa…" March 20, 1902. Napa County Newspaper Archive.
United States Census Bureau. "Urban and Rural Areas." www.census.gov/history/www/programs/geography/urban_and_rural_areas.html.

Bibliography

Mrs. Tobin's Restaurants

Napa County Reporter. "Mrs. Mary Tobin." May 31, 1878. California State Library.
———. "Refreshment Saloon." February 7, 1879. California State Library.
Napa Journal. "Appointed Guardian." January 30, 1910. Napa County Newspaper Archive.
———. "Death of Michael Tobin." April 19, 1898. Napa County Newspaper Archive.
———. "Mrs. M. Tobin." June 8, 1883. Napa County Newspaper Archive.
———. "Mrs. M. Tobin…" May 26, 1893. Napa County Newspaper Archive.
———. "Mrs. Tobin Has Sold Out." December 24, 1892. Napa County Newspaper Archive.
———. "Mrs. Tobin Makes a Fine Display…" April 19, 1898. Napa County Newspaper Archive.
———. "Mrs. Tobin Returns." November 5, 1902. Napa County Newspaper Archive.
———. "Mrs. Tobin's Restaurant." August 20, 1890. Napa County Newspaper Archive.
———. "Mrs. Tobin's Restaurant." August 6, 1893. Napa County Newspaper Archive.
———. "Tom McGill Goes East." September 4, 1897. Napa County Newspaper Archive.

Classic Grill

Mulgrew, Jeanette. Interview by Alexandria Brown. June 5, 2019.
Napa Journal. "Classic Grill." July 7, 1927. Napa County Newspaper Archive.
———. "Classic Grill." May 13, 1930. Napa County Newspaper Archive.
———. "Classic Owners Thank Patrons." September 19, 1934. Napa County Newspaper Archive.
———. "Fine Property Purchased by Dan Smernes." August 5, 1927. Napa County Newspaper Archive.
———. "'Golden Glow Inn' Opens Tomorrow." August 22, 1933. Napa County Newspaper Archive.
———. "Meet 'Bull Montana' at Pete's Grill." June 7, 1930. Napa County Newspaper Archive.

BIBLIOGRAPHY

———. "Old Name Resumed by Restaurant." January 26, 1936. Napa County Newspaper Archive.

———. "Sum Involved in Transfer of Napa Hotel Not Revealed." May 13, 1936. Napa County Newspaper Archive.

———. "There Are No Hard Times When You Eat at the Classic Grill." February 14, 1931. Napa County Newspaper Archive.

———. "Vallejo Scene of Murder." November 4, 1927. Napa County Newspaper Archive.

———. "We Serve Fresh Crabs and Lobsters Every Day." March 12, 1931. Napa County Newspaper Archive.

Napa Register. "Drowns While on Honeymoon." December 11, 1923. Napa County Newspaper Archive.

———. "Found Guilty of Murder of Former Napan." December 16, 1927. Napa County Newspaper Archive.

———. "Hennessey Block Has Been Sold." August 4, 1927. Napa County Newspaper Archive.

———. "Infant Daughter Is Taken by Death." September 24, 1923. Napa County Newspaper Archive.

———. "Menu for Sunday Dinner at 'Classic Grill.'" May 20, 1922. Napa County Newspaper Archive.

———. "Nick Smernes, Brother of Dan Smernes of Napa, Dies Suddenly in Berkeley." April 26, 1926. Napa County Newspaper Archive.

———. "'Pete' and 'Nick' Both Married While in Greece." April 16, 1929. Napa County Newspaper Archive.

———. "Pete's Grill Is Open for Business." February 8, 1930. Napa County Newspaper Archive.

———. "Smernes Back at Classic Grill." August 27, 1935. Napa County Newspaper Archive.

———. "Special Sunday Chicken Dinner, $1." June 3, 1922. Napa County Newspaper Archive.

Sacramento Union. "To the Creditors of Crystal Restaurant…" December 16, 1911. California Digital Newspaper Collection.

PART VIII. MID-CENTURY MODERN

Bentley, Jeanine, and Linda Kantor. "Food Availability (Per Capita) Data System." USDA. Last updated August 26, 2019. www.ers.usda.gov/data-products/food-availability-per-capita-data-system.

BIBLIOGRAPHY

Edge, John T. *Hamburgers and Fries: An American Story*. New York: G.P. Putnam's Sons, 2005.

Smith, Andrew F. *Hamburger: A Global History*. London: Reaktion Books, 2008.

Specht, Joshua. *Red Meat Republic: A Hoof-to-Table History of How Beef Changed America*. Princeton, NJ: Princeton University Press, 2019.

Wilson, Lowell L., K.G. MacDonald, H.H. Mayo and K.J. Drewry. "Development of the Beef Cattle Industry." *Historical Documents of the Purdue Cooperative Extension Service*. 1965. Paper 3. docs.lib.purdue.edu/anrhist/3.

Jonesy's Famous Steak House

Bridgeford, Richard Atherton. *Living the High Life*. West Conshohocken, PA: Infinity Publishing, 2004.

Calistogan. "Jonesy's Famous Steak House." June 25, 1964. Napa County Newspaper Archive.

Carson, L. Pierce. "Airport Chie Partain Retiring." *Napa Register*, February 23, 1987. Napa County Newspaper Archive.

Courtney, Kevin. "Jonesy's Restaurant a 50-Year Tradition." *Napa Register*, October 6, 1996. Napa County Newspaper Archive.

Dorgan, Marsha. "Jonesy's Means Business When It Comes to Lunch." *Napa Register*, July 3, 1998. Napa County Newspaper Archive.

Dunn, Bernice. "150,000 Use Napa Airport Annually." *Napa Journal*, December 11, 1958. Napa County Newspaper Archive.

Egneckow. "Napa Flight School to End Operations After 40 Years." *North Bay Business Journal*, February 22, 2012. www.northbaybusinessjournal.com.

Ernst, Doug. "County Supervisors Seeking Jonesy's Expansion Answers." *Napa Register*, January 18, 1984. Napa County Newspaper Archive.

Ezettie, Louis. "Looking into Napa's Past and Present." *Napa Register*, January 15, 1977. Napa County Newspaper Archive.

Ford, Jim. "Napa As It Was." *Napa Register*, January 4, 2010. Napa County Newspaper Archive.

Game, Ross P. "New Secretary on the Job." *Napa Register*, April 14, 1965. Napa County Newspaper Archive.

Healey, Beverly Brown. E-mail to Alexandra Brown. August 1, 2019.

Huffman, Jennifer. "Japan Airlines to Leave Napa." *Napa Register*, June 15, 2010. Napa County Newspaper Archive.

Kennedy, Mike. "Good Food Is My Line." *Napa Register*, July 11, 1974. Napa County Newspaper Archive.

Bibliography

Napa Register. "Early Vacation for Jones Due to Meat." August 29, 1973. Napa County Newspaper Archive.

———. "Fire Levels Airport Building." May 28, 1952. Napa County Newspaper Archive.

———. "Hugh Jones Dies." January 7, 1977. Napa County Newspaper Archive.

———. "Hugh Jones Jr." October 12, 1989. Napa County Newspaper Archive.

———. "Jonesy's Famous Steak House." May 26, 1953. Napa County Newspaper Archive.

———. "Mrs. Jones, 57, Victim of Cancer." July 31, 1967. Napa County Newspaper Archive.

———. "The Phantom Fork." August 8, 2006. Napa County Newspaper Archive.

———. "TV Sketch Features Jonesy's." February 7, 1970. Napa County Newspaper Archive.

———. "A West Coast Favorite for Excellent Cuisine." July 30, 19760. Napa County Newspaper Archive.

———. "Work Passes Midway Mark on New County Airport Building." April 6, 1953. Napa County Newspaper Archive.

Stanley, Pat. "Born of War." *Napa Register*, October 6, 1996. Napa County Newspaper Archive.

Stouffer, Pat. "Mother's First Small Plane Flight." *Napa Register*, July 2, 1966. Napa County Newspaper Archive.

Trademarkia. "Strestcrete Trademark Information: Basalt Rock Company, Inc." trademark.trademarkia.com/strestcrete-71565036.html.

Wyman, Alisha. "Jonesy's Memories: Locals Look Back Fondly on Iconic Napa Restaurant." *Napa Register*, December 6, 2009. Napa County Newspaper Archive.

———. "Keeping Up with Jonesy's." *Napa Register*, December 6, 2009. Napa County Newspaper Archive.

Taylor's Refresher

Averill, Charles V., Oliver E. Bowen Jr., Fenelon F. Davis, Clarence A. Logan, Louis A. Norman Jr., John C. O'Brien, Reid J. Sampson, Richard M. Steward, Henry H. Symons and William E. Ver Planck. *The Counties of California: Mineral Resources and Mineral Production During 1947*. Bulletin 142. July 1949. archive.org/details/countiesofca194700calirich.

BIBLIOGRAPHY

Calistogan. "McGill Rock and Sand Company." May 24, 1956. Napa County Newspaper Archive.

Carson, L. Pierce. "The Great American Cheeseburger." *Napa Register*, May 29, 2001. Napa County Newspaper Archive.

Huffman, Jennifer. "Battle Over Branding Taylor's." *St. Helena Star*, April 1, 2010. Napa County Newspaper Archive.

Napa Register. "The '50s Live Again at Taylor's Refresher." May 30, 2003. Napa County Newspaper Archive.

———. "Lloyd Taylor." August 16, 1989. Napa County Newspaper Archive.

Nicholson, Jean Taylor, and Tom Nicholson. Phone interview by Alexandria Brown. April 2, 2019.

Parker, Robert. "Robert Parker's Most Memorable Meals of 1999." *The Wine Advocate* 126 (2000). St. Helena Wine Library.

Ricketts, A.H. "Manner of Locating and Holding Mineral Claims in California." *California Journal of Mines and Geology* 44, no. 1 (January 1948). archive.org/details/californiajourna44cali.

Sams, Reid. "Zagar Signs Mark Valley's Entrances." *St. Helena Star*, June 5, 1986. Napa County Newspaper Archive.

St. Helena Star. "City Council to Continue Budget Sessions Today." August 19, 1982. Napa County Newspaper Archive.

———. "Fresh Corn…" August 15, 1968. Napa County Newspaper Archive.

———. "It's Time for Us to Crow About Our Products." January 23, 1964. Napa County Newspaper Archive.

———. "Pictured Here Are Phases of the Project…" October 3, 1947. Napa County Newspaper Archive.

———. "Planning Commission Turns Down Development Proposal." February 8, 1973. Napa County Newspaper Archive.

———. "St. Helena's Newest Business Enterprise…" June 22, 1950. Napa County Newspaper Archive.

———. "Stop!" August 8, 1957. Napa County Newspaper Archive.

———. "Stop at Taylor's Refresher." July 18, 1957. Napa County Newspaper Archive.

———. "Thick Vanilla Shake." September 29, 1960. Napa County Newspaper Archive.

———. "We Want to Express…" January 30, 1964. Napa County Newspaper Archive.

———. "You Are Cordially Invited…" June 22, 1950. Napa County Newspaper Archive.

BIBLIOGRAPHY

Talley, Marilee. "Planners—Main Street No Place for Bocce Ball." *St. Helena Star*, April 4, 1991. Napa County Newspaper Archive.

Palby's

Dorgan, Marsha. "Palby's." *Napa Register*, December 1, 2002. Napa County Newspaper Archive.
DuCharme, Darlene. "Residents Rank Canyon Cuisine." *Napa Register*, April 6, 1994. Napa County Newspaper Archive.
Katzanek, Jack. "Fire Update: Palby's Hopes to Reopen by Weekend." *Napa Register*, March 30, 1992. Napa County Newspaper Archive.
Keegan, Roseann. "AmCan Icon Closes Its Doors." *Napa Register*, October 10, 2003. Napa County Newspaper Archive.
Luippold, Linda. "Cast in Cement: American Canyon's Industrial Past." *American Canyon Eagle*, April 26, 2005. Napa County Newspaper Archive.
Meredith, Diana. "American Canyon Restaurant Burns." *Napa Register*, March 28, 1992. Napa County Newspaper Archive.
Miller, Sharon. Letter to the editor. *Napa Register*, October 21, 2003. Napa County Newspaper Archive.
Napa Register. "Attention American Canyon Voters." October 28, 1981. Napa County Newspaper Archive.
———. "Civil Rights Suit Filed for 'Refusal.'" March 23, 1960. Napa County Newspaper Archive.
———. "Clemence S. Freskan." August 24, 1972. Napa County Newspaper Archive.
———. "For Sale or for Rent." September 7, 1933. Napa County Newspaper Archive.
———. "John Freskan." March 3, 1959. Napa County Newspaper Archive.
———. "No Finer Foods Anywhere." March 11, 1966. Napa County Newspaper Archive.
———. "One of the Few Sea Lions…" June 6, 1964. Napa County Newspaper Archive.
———. "Palby's Reopens." April 6, 1992. Napa County Newspaper Archive.
———. "Palby's Tempts Palate and Purse." March 22, 1985. Napa County Newspaper Archive.
Neave, Charles. "This Old Restaurant a Rare Bird." *Napa Register*, January 4, 1993. Napa County Newspaper Archive.

Sherlock, Paulette Freskan. Letter to the editor. *Napa Register*, October 15, 1981. Napa County Newspaper Archive.

Zito, Kelly. "Napa-Sonoma Marsh Restoration's Last Phase Begins." *San Francisco Chronicle*, August 26, 2010. www.sfgate.com.

PART IX. RESTAURANT RENAISSANCE

Carson, L. Pierce. "In Yountville, Every Restaurant Is Unique." *Napa Register*, April 23, 1980. Napa County Newspaper Archive.

———. "Next—The Wine with Food List." *Napa Register*, April 9, 1983. Napa County Newspaper Archive.

Courtney, Kevin. "The Restaurant Boom." *Napa Register*, April 5, 1980. Napa County Newspaper Archive.

Magnolia Hotel (Yountville)

Alexander, Pat. *Yountville*. Charleston, SC: Arcadia Press, 2009.

Andrews, Peter, and George Allen. *Country Inns of America: California, a Guide to the Inns of California*. Los Angeles: Knapp Press, 1980.

Bowen, Marie. "Guy Fling: George Yount's Guide." Napa County Historical Society. Last modified June 18, 2016. napahistory.org.

Caldewey, Jeffrey. *Wine Tour: Napa Valley*. St. Helena, CA: Vintage Image, 1979.

Calistogian. "Sheriff Raids a Hotel at Yountville, Makes Arrests." November 19, 1920. Napa County Newspaper Archive.

———. "T.B. Hopper…" March 10, 1899. Napa County Newspaper Archive.

Gorman, Tom. Letter to the editor. *Napa Register*, September 14, 1978. Napa County Newspaper Archive.

Graffin, Craig. Interview by Alexandria Brown. August 14, 2019.

Holt, John. "Yountville: The Beginnings." Napa County Historical Society. Last modified February 19, 2015. napahistory.org.

Napa Journal. "Building Given to 4-H Club for Future Meetings." June 26, 1937. Napa County Newspaper Archive.

———. "P. Guillaume…" May 24, 1896. Napa County Newspaper Archive.

Napa Register. "Magnolia Hotel Adds Gourmet Restaurant." November 26, 1973. Napa County Newspaper Archive.

BIBLIOGRAPHY

———. "Magnolia Hotel Reopens." March 14, 1977. Napa County Newspaper Archive.
———. "Magnolia Owner Still Plans Opening Despite 'Red Tag.'" November 29, 1973. Napa County Newspaper Archive.
———. "Man Is Found Dead in Bed at Yountville." April 16, 1936. Napa County Newspaper Archive.
———. "Napa County Health Officer Closes Yountville Hotel." April 18, 1936. Napa County Newspaper Archive.
———. "Volstead Act." March 30, 1921. Napa County Newspaper Archive.
Paulsen, Sasha. "A Decade of Food." *Napa Register*, January 4, 2010. Napa County Newspaper Archive.
———. "Zare Shuts Its Doors." *Napa Register*, July 27, 2007. Napa County Newspaper Archive.
St. Helena Star. "The German Bakery." January 16, 1891. Napa County Newspaper Archive.
———. "A New Resort." August 14, 1903. Napa County Newspaper Archive.
———. "P. Guillaume…" November 1, 1895. Napa County Newspaper Archive.
Woodside, Peter. "Calistoga: Born-Again Community." *Napa Register*, August 11, 1984. Napa County Newspaper Archive.

RECIPES

Coss, John. "Clear Fish Chowder." *Napa Register*, November 15, 1989. Napa County Newspaper Archive.
D., Sarah. "Eds Household…" *Sacramento Union*, February 10, 1877. California Digital Newspaper Collection.
De Lazzer, Maryellen. "Scalloped Potatoes and Wieners Are Easy to Cook, Easy to Eat Says Mrs. Frank De Lazzer." *Napa Journal*, November 19, 1950. Napa County Newspaper Archive.
Franco, Miguel. "Stuffed Pasilla Chiles." *Napa Register*, November 15, 1989. Napa County Newspaper Archive.
Glin, Hervé. "Starmont Restaurant." *Napa Register*, November 15, 1989. Napa County Newspaper Archive.
Il cuoco senza pretese ossia la cucina facile ed economica. Vol. 1. 2nd ed. Italy: C. Pietro. Ostinelli, 1826. books.google.com/books?id=rlxeHAAACAAJ.

Bibliography

Independent Calistogian. "Mutton Chops." November 11, 1880. Napa County Newspaper Archive.

Napa Journal. "Chili Sauce." September 16, 1917. Napa County Newspaper Archive.

———. "Household Recipes." July 30, 1892. Napa County Newspaper Archive.

———. "How to Stew Oysters." December 17, 1885. Napa County Newspaper Archive.

———. "Ice Cream with Variations." August 15, 1900. Napa County Newspaper Archive.

Napa Register. "Cooking Hints from Abroad Give Zest to Dishes Here." July 24, 1931. Napa County Newspaper Archive.

Nichelini, Caterina. *Caterina's Parmesan Polenta.* Nichelini Family Winery, 2019.

Richards, Paul. "Three Recipes for Chop Suey." In *The Lunch Room*, 78–79. Chicago: Hotel Monthly, 1911. books.google.com/books?id=Fo45AQAAMAAJ.

St. Helena Star. "Breakfast Biscuit." September 25, 1875. Napa County Newspaper Archive.

———. "Mrs. Adam's Wedding Cake." October 29, 1875. Napa County Newspaper Archive.

Tamburelli, Theresa. "Venison Saute." *Napa Register*, October 30, 1954. Napa County Newspaper Archive.

Wilson, Judith. "Tasty Dishes for Today." *Napa Journal*, August 1, 1934. Napa County Newspaper Archive.

Index

A

A-1 Cafe 87, 89, 109
Aetna Springs Resort 53
Alfredo's 97
American Hotel 37, 43
Arcade Restaurant 29, 31
Arcade Saloon 25
Asia Cafe 91

B

Basalt Rock Company 130
Baxter, Turner G. 22, 23
Bear Flag Revolt 15, 16
Berlin Cafe 111
Blumer, Jacob 19
Boyd, Sam 70
Brannan, Samuel 17, 49, 50
Brooklyn Hotel 97, 102
Budo 158

C

California Restaurant 111
Calistoga Hotel 52
Calistoga Hot Springs 17, 49
Capitani, John 108
Capitol Saloon 19
Carriage House Restaurant 158
Carrvajal, Inez 69
Cavagnaro family 95, 102, 109, 129
Celadon 158
Chan, Shuck 80
Chanterelle 158, 160
Cheong, Jew 87, 88
Chesebro, Jane 49, 50
Chesebro, John 49, 50, 51
Chicago 18, 117
Chic's Burgers 127
Child, Julia 155, 158
China Cafe 91
Cittoni, Clemente 105, 106
Classic Grill 117

INDEX

Cole's Chop House 158
Compadres Rio Grille 74
Coombs, Nathan 15, 16, 17, 37, 43
Culinary Institute of America 158

D

Dabner, Frank 67, 68
Dabner, Manuel 67, 68
Daglia, Louis and Erminia 107, 109
Delmonico Spanish Chop House 64
Depot Hotel 99
Depot Saloon. *See* Depot Hotel
Dorr, Matthias 19, 20, 21
Downtown Joe's 113

E

Eagle Hotel 152
Eglin, Eugene 42
El Cafe Talpita 74
El Faro Restaurant 72
Elite Saloon 25
Empire Saloon 17, 37, 159
Espinosa, Miguel "Mike" 69
Exchange Restaurant 24, 39, 41

F

Feliz, Peter 64
Ferroggiaro, Giovanni Baptista "G.B." 99
Ferroggiaro, Virginia 99, 100, 101
Fimby, George 63
Fimby, Trinidad 63

Fountain Restaurant 30
Fred's Chili Bowl 107
French Laundry 158
French Restaurant 39, 41
Freskan, Peter 144, 146, 147

G

Garcia, Juana 64, 65
German Bakery 152
German House 84
Golden Dragon 91
gold rush 13, 18, 19, 67, 69, 87
Gott, Duncan 141
Gott, Joel 141
Gott's Roadside. *See* Taylor's Refresher
Grand Hotel 33
Groezinger, Gottlob 151
Guillaume, Pierre "Peter" 152

H

Harbin, James 43
Hatton, Edward and Sabina 31
Hatton, Margaret E. 31
Heibel, George 55, 56
Hernandez, Carlota "Lottie" 69
Hernandez, Gregorio and Carmen 72
Highway 29 Cafe 127
Higuera, Nicolás 15, 17, 65
Hogan, Ellen 43, 45, 46
Hogan, John 23, 41, 43, 44, 45
Hogan, Patrick Milton 29, 30

INDEX

I

Imperial Tamale Parlor 66, 67

J

Javon, A. 25
Jew Cheong 109
Jones, Ethel 129, 130, 132
Jones, Hugh 129, 130, 133
Jonesy's Famous Steak House 129
Juárez, Cayetano 15, 60, 70, 100, 143
Juárez, María 60

K

Kenny's Drive-In 127
Kilburn, Ralph 16, 17
Kin Lim 79, 80
Knotty Pine Drive-In 127

L

Lai Hing Company 79, 83
Lande, John Baptiste 152, 158
La Placita 75
Lee, Albert 87, 91
Lily's Drive-In 127
Locken, Bonnie 155
Locken, Bruce 155, 158
Low, Yuen 87, 88

M

Magnolia Hotel (Calistoga) 39, 49, 159
Magnolia Hotel (Yountville) 151, 152, 159
Maldonado, John and Ruth 108
Mare Island Naval Station 129
Marino's Grill 111
Marion, Frances 55
McClenic, Jeannie 145
McGill Rock and Sand Company 135
McGill, Tom 114
Monmert, Achille 20
Moore, Harry. *See* Mower, E. Harry
Mower, E. Harry 23, 24, 41
Mrs. Tobin's Restaurant 113, 159

N

Napa Delicatessen 48, 107
Napa Hotel 31, 39, 41, 43, 44, 89, 107, 119, 122
Napa Motel 109
Napa Raviola Parlor and Noodle Parlor 107
Napa Restaurant 23, 39, 41, 43
Napa Valley Opera House 89, 91, 119
New York City 18, 25, 29, 88
Nichols, J.E. "Nick" 49
Nielsen, John 32, 33
Nielsen, M. 32, 33
Nielsen's Restaurant 33
Nu Way Drug Fountain 127

O

Olds, Annie 65, 66
Owens, Len D. 54, 55
Owyeong, Henry 87, 91
Oxbow Public Market 158

P

Palace Hotel 101
Palby's 143, 144
Paris Restaurant 21
Patwin, Southern 15, 59, 60, 143
Pete's Grill 119
Pierce, Harrison 16, 17

Q

Quijada, Edward 69, 70

R

Railroad House (St. Helena) 25
Reams, Charles 70, 84
Reeder's Calistoga Maid Creamery and Restaurant 74
Revere House 20, 49, 114
Ritchie, James C. 30
Roux, Lucien 42
Ruffino's 97
Russ House 84, 86

S

Sacramento 81, 117, 122, 130
San Francisco 17, 30, 32, 42, 69, 77, 87, 101, 104, 141, 143, 152
Shanghai Low 48
Silkes, Manull (Manuel) 65, 66
Smernes, Daniel 117, 122
Smernes, Olga 117, 122
Smernes, Pete 117, 119
Sonoma County 15, 60, 67, 151
Soscol House 37
Spanish-American Chop House 64
Speero's 159
Standard Portland Cement 143
Starmont Restaurant 160
St. Helena Restaurant 32, 33
Stuky, John 64
Swiss Union Hotel 152

T

Tacos Chavez 74
Tamburelli, Theresa 101, 103
Taylor, Lloyd "Popsie" 136, 140
Taylor, Marion 135
Taylor's Automatic Refresher. *See* Taylor's Refresher
Taylor's Refresher 135
Tobin, Mary 113, 116
Toogood, Charley 138, 140
True's Saloon 31

U

Union Hotel 102

V

Vallejo, Mariano 15, 143, 151
Vallejo, Salvador 15, 61, 143
Valley House Restaurant 22, 23, 41
Van Loon, Paul 50
Villa Romano 37

W

Wappo 15, 59, 60, 151
Washington Hotel 99
White House 152
Wong, Ming "Alfred" 87, 89
Wong's House of Chop Suey 91
Wo, Sang 84, 85

Y

Yount, George 143, 151

Z

Zaré 158

About the Author

Alexandria Brown grew up in Napa. She has a master's in library and information science and a master's in U.S. history. She is a teen services librarian by day, a writer and reviewer by night and a local historian by passion. In everything she does, diversity, equity and inclusion are at the forefront. Her first book, *Hidden History of Napa Valley*, shares the stories of the marginalized communities that helped make Napa the world-famous region it is today. Alexandria lives in the North Bay with her pet rats and ever-increasing piles of books. She can be found on Twitter (@QueenOfRats), Instagram (@bookjockeyalex) and her blog (bookjockeyalex.com).

Visit us at
www.historypress.com

www.ingramcontent.com/pod-product-compliance
Lightning Source LLC
Chambersburg PA
CBHW042139160426
43201CB00021B/2340